ME(

When I met Emmy, I was exiting my first business and was on the early part of building a career portfolio of Build-Advise-Invest as Emmy recommends. In MegaWealth, Emmy shares the Silicon Valley Secret of building wealth by creating network effects between the 3 elements of your career: Build, Advise, and Invest. This is not known to many people outside of Silicon Valley. MegaWealth lays out the many ways to do this in an easy to read and actionable format.

- Mrunalini Parvataneni, MD, Chief Medical Officer, Optina Diagnostics, Senior Advisor, Boston Consulting Group, Expert in Residence, DigitalDx Ventures

"Asymmetrical upside. I may not have thought about it much, but after reading Emmy's first book, it's what occupies all of my thoughts today. No matter what stage of career you're in, if you want to be in a position for near-limitless upside, you're holding the playbook. Every path in life has some element of risk, you may as well choose the paths that have exponentially more reward."

- Jonathan Cronstedt, Board Director and Former President, Kajabi, www.jcron.com

Emmy highlights the benefits of generating wealth by creating network effects between 3 elements of your career: Build, Advise, and Invest. By thoughtfully designing your career with this type of portfolio approach, you can increase your chances of building significant wealth — and make your career even more fulfilling. –

- **Karen Roter Davis, Managing Partner, Entrada Ventures, Former Google Executive, Former Startup Executive, and Independent Board Member & Advisor**

Emmy's first book showed me the path of leverage and changed the trajectory of my career. With a successful start of a career in enterprise software & tech sales, I knew I needed to make the jump to Building Equity. MegaWealth is next level. It moves you from concept to strategy to execution. Emmy lays out the path brilliantly.

- **Dan Kunze, Senior Director, Americas Sales, LeoLabs, Vice Chairman of the Board, Task Force Movement, and Limited Partner, Stony Lonesome Group LLC**

Emmy has given me career advice for over a decade. In that time, I've generated wealth from investing, advising, and building. I co-founded and sold my own company in my 30s. I am living proof that building equity early from multiple sources works!

- **Greg Magadini, Director of Derivatives, Amberdata, Former CEO and Founder, Genesis Volatility, and Investor**

MEGAWEALTH

MEGAWEALTH

ESCAPE THE BROKE UPPER CLASS, SUPERCHARGE YOUR LUCK, AND TRANSFORM YOURSELF FROM KNOWLEDGE WORKER TO INDUSTRY TITAN

Emmy Sobieski, CFA

My10Min LLC
Wellington, FL

Publisher's Cataloging-In-Publication-Data:
Names: Sobieski, Emmy, author
Title: MegaWealth: Escape the Broke Upper Class, Supercharge Your Luck, and Transform Yourself from Knowledge Worker to Industry Titan./ Emmy Sobieski
Description: Wellington, FL, My10Min LLC
Identifiers: ISBN 979-8-9894108-5-9 (Hardback) | 979-8-9894108-3-5 (Paperback) | 979-8-9894108-6-6 (Kindle) | 979-8-9894108-7-3 (Audible)
Subjects: LCSH: Wealth | Occupations | Investing | Vocational Guidance | Boards of Directors | Boards, Advisory | Private Equity | Venture Capital | Finance

Disclaimers: This book is for informational purposes only. It is not intended to serve as a substitute for professional advice. The author and publisher specifically disclaim any and all liability arising directly or indirectly from the use of any information contained in this book and make no guarantees to the results you'll achieve by reading this book. All business requires risk and hard work. The conversations in the book are based on the author's recollection and retold in a way to communicate the meaning of what was said. The results and client case studies presented in this book represent results achieved working directly with the author. Your results may vary when undertaking any new business venture or investing strategy.

To my talented clients, I wrote this book for you.

I'm honored by your trust, awestruck by your boldness, and excited for your future! My greatest joy is seeing you bet on yourself and achieve your (previously "impossible") dreams.

Go for it!

"Once I saw my map, I couldn't unsee it.

Suddenly, no other path made sense." - Trusted Client

"Somebody's going to make BIG money. It might as well be us!"

- My (former) Hedge Fund Boss

CONTENTS

INTRODUCTION

Why Did I Write MegaWealth?

There are 25,000 self-made families in the US worth over $100 million, and I can show you how to become one.

This book exists so you can map your unique wealth path to join the 25,000 self-made families worth over $100 million in the US...without needing to come from families with connections, to know people, or be born in Silicon Valley or NYC.

The next $100-millionaires shouldn't just be those who knew someone in New York or Silicon Valley and grew up hearing stories of Wall Street, board directors, venture capital, and private equity around the dinner table. You don't need to be from a certain family or region, but you do need to know the paths, start early enough, work hard, and have some talent and luck.

You'll be amazed at how much luck and serendipity start flowing your way when you know what to look for (and continue to work hard). This happens because you are confident in the path you have mapped out for yourself!

I have mentored many underprivileged students to millions by age 30, witnessed multiple friends from modest backgrounds make $100 million by age 50, and worked closely for years with five billionaires. I share this mindset and experience with you so you'll build confidence and feel like part of the inner circle. This book shows you the way to $100 million and beyond, no matter your background.

When people think about wealth, they think about investing, yet the most important investment isn't a stock. Your most important investment is your career. In this book, I will show you how to multiply your chances at big wealth by architecting your career and investing in one, cohesive strategy.

My first book, *MegaWealth: Careers*, describes 5 potential career paths to MegaWealth, $100 million+, and there are more.

After writing *MegaWealth: Careers*, the #1 question I got from readers was how to execute on those careers. This book is my answer to this important question. In MegaWealth, I show you how to navigate the transitions between the 3Bs (Breaking In, Building Equity, and Breaking Out) and how to build a personal money flywheel (earning simultaneously from building, advising, and investing).

MegaWealth shows you how to navigate those paths to reach MegaWealth, i.e. $50M or $100 million or more, by making the best choices during the most critical transitions in your career.

The Outcomes of The Book

Using the PDF MegaWealth Workbook, available for download in Chapter 15: Resources, you'll map your potential path to $100 million in wealth, know what you'll need to do, know what will need to go right for you, and know how hard you'll need to work.

You'll learn to use the 3Bs Framework to exit the Broke Upper Class by separating your time from your wealth creation. People who are part of the Broke Upper Class are everywhere. They drive cars and live in houses they can barely afford. They're stuck in the Breaking In phase of their careers, earning a bit more each year, with their time spent tied to the money they earn.

You'll see a path to exiting the Breaking In phase in favor of Building Equity which can create step-function increases in your wealth by separating your time from your wealth creation.

Speaking of step-function wealth increases, you'll learn how to build your own MegaWealth Money Flywheel (and what it is and why it works). You'll then learn how to apply the MegaWealth Pyramid audit to remove any potential obstacles to your success. These tools will help you moonshot your career and wealth to heights you never dreamed were possible.

The big Silicon Valley Secret is the money flywheel. While it is critical you know where you are and where you want to go using the 3Bs Framework (Breaking In, Building Equity, and Breaking Out), designing and executing on your money flywheel as you move into the Building Equity phase will be the single most important move you can make to significantly increase your chance at reaching MegaWealth or more.

Finally, you'll build your own personal MegaWealth Plan using the downloadable PDF MegaWealth Workbook (in Chapter 15: Resources). With your own personal plan, you'll feel a deep, energetic motivation and purpose on your unique path to MegaWealth.

MegaWealth #1 Takeaway

My hope is you see what is possible for you, that you'll read this book and believe in yourself, and that you'll suddenly see a clear path to your goals. And those goals? What was once a dream you barely dared to share can become a concrete (yet flexible) map to your $100 million (or more) in wealth.

MegaWealth isn't just about earning more. It's about realizing your highest potential and knowing your purpose so you can use your wealth and power to have the impact you desire. This is why we spend time aligning your values with the path you'll take. When you arrive, those values will help you decide the kind of impact you want to have with your wealth.

If you use my 3Bs Framework (Break In, Build Equity, and Break Out) to build your 3-pronged personal Money Flywheel (Build, Advise, Invest), you'll increase your chances at reaching MegaWealth faster and with fewer detours or roadblocks.

What if I Want More Help Building My Plan?

This book contains everything you need to know to build your MegaWealth Plan. However, some clients like to speed up their results while benefiting from the situations and mindsets I have been exposed to after working for 5 billionaires and seeing multiple people make over $100 million by age 50. If you want help customizing your own MegaWealth Plan with individual reflections on your situation, give me a call. Here's the link: https://calendly.com/emmy-sobieski/15-minute-intro-call

Don't worry. I've held nothing back in writing this book. It contains all my best ideas. You'll be learning a lot throughout these pages, and I will be here for you when you are ready to take the next step. I'm here to get you the results you want.

Just by taking the time to read this book and think about your career, you are ahead of 99% of your peers. I'm so honored you are joining me on this journey. Let's get started!

- Emmy

PART 1: MOVE FROM KNOWLEDGE WORKER TO INDUSTRY TITAN. SEPARATING TIME SPENT FROM WEALTH CREATED

CHAPTER 1: A NEW REALITY

You are working on interesting things with fascinating and brilliant people while building wealth far faster than when you were solely a salaried employee feeling like part of the Broke Upper Class. Now, your wealth and connections enable you to have the positive impact you want on your family, community, and world. This legacy is yours to design and create.

While you work each day, your multiple positions give you more shots at millions in wealth, and as those liquidity events arrive, you can then compound those into more wealth. Your positions as a board member, fund partner, and startup executive mean you are networking in the highest echelons, setting you up for even more lucrative opportunities.

And the funny thing? While you are busy, it doesn't feel like hard work. You are having more fun and working on more interesting projects than your friends who are still stuck in your old life, the Broke Upper Class.

How did you get here? Following the 3Bs Framework, you moved from the Breaking In phase to Building Equity. You activated your Money Flywheel: you are in a P&L leadership position at a fast-growing startup, have 1-2 board seats, and earn carry (a type of equity pay) as a part-time partner at a PE fund or VC fund.

Seem too good to be true? I have made hundreds of millions for my billionaire bosses, witnessed multiple close friends make MegaWealth by age 50, and mentored multiple underprivileged students to make millions by age 30 on their way to MegaWealth. What is the biggest factor I've seen in peers, bosses, and, more broadly, in Silicon Valley that can increase your chances at achieving this wealth? The Money Flywheel.

Let's check out some examples.

Case Studies Showing 3Bs' Money Flywheel in Action

Marc Andreessen - Create Exits Early and Often

Marc Andreessen is the "classic" case of hitting startup fortunes through great timing (right time, right place for the emergence of the commercial internet), a brilliant mind, and a willingness to take risks. He went to one of the top technical universities in the world, the University of Illinois at Urbana–Champaign, where in his senior year he learned about the world wide web (www) standard for the internet and started working to create its first browser, Mosaic. While in school, he also worked on technologies related to Silicon Graphics' software.

When Andreessen moved to California, he was introduced to the former founder and CEO of Silicon Graphics, Jim Clark. They decided to found a company (Netscape) to help people browse the internet using the www standard. Thanks to having the right solution at the right time in a hot space, a mere 2.5 years after graduating college, Andreessen's Netscape went public via IPO in 1996. In 1998, Andreessen sold 25% of his stake in Netscape for over $7 million. In 1999, AOL purchased Netscape for $4.2 billion (the deal was eventually consummated at $10 billion), giving Andreessen a massive liquidity event.

Selling his first startup 6 years after college graduation was just a warm up.

With Ben Horowitz, Andreessen founded and sold Opsware to Hewlett-Packard for $1.6 billion. Following his entrepreneurial journey, he founded Venture Capital firm, Andreessen Horowitz, with the idea that the best founders would want investors who had been founders themselves. Completing his money flywheel

(Build, Invest, and Advise), Marc Andreessen served on the boards of eBay, Facebook, Oculus VR, Hewlett-Packard Enterprise, and many more.

Lessons: (1) Do your research, know what's hot, what's next, and participate. (2) Create liquidity events early and often, then compound them. (3) Build your own money flywheel (see Chapters 4, 6, 8, and 12) to increase the surface area of your opportunities. Your network drives your net worth!

Peter Thiel - Billionaire Regrets

Peter Theil is the founder of Paypal, Palantir Technologies, Founders Fund, and the Thiel Fellowship. He was the first outside investor in Facebook. In 2023, his net worth approached $10 billion. Yet, his fellowship is a window into his regrets. As opposed to Marc Andreessen, who IPO'd his first company 2.5 years after graduating college, Thiel spent 9 years in preparation, 9 years locked in the Breaking In phase of his career.

He grew up in Silicon Valley, graduating from Stanford in 1989. He then got both his JD and MBA from Stanford. After that, Thiel worked as a securities lawyer at Sullivan & Cromwell, as a speechwriter for former U.S. Secretary of Education William Bennett, and later as a derivatives trader at Credit Suisse. While he was building impressive experiences and accolades, he was stuck in the Breaking In phase of his career far longer than Marc Andreessen.

In 1998, nine years after graduating college, Thiel co-founded PayPal. He sold it to eBay in 2002 for $1.2 billion. Now, his Thiel Fellowship pays college students to drop out and work on their ideas. He's encouraging others to move faster into the Building Equity phase than he did.

Lessons: (1) The time in Breaking In should be as long as necessary and as short as possible. (2) The network you build can become your greatest asset (hat tip: "PayPal Mafia"). (3) Most billionaires see ways they could do it even better if they had the chance at a do-over.

Both Marc Andreessen and Peter Theil are billionaires who went through the 3Bs (Breaking In, Building Equity, Breaking Out) and built their own money flywheels (Build, Invest, Advise). Now, I'll share some case studies showing that you don't have to found your own startup or even work at a startup. You can find a plan that builds in tons of financial upside and also fits with your personality.

Bill Gurley - Man With A Plan

I met Bill Gurley when he was in the middle of executing his plan. His success was inevitable. He wasn't from Silicon Valley, and his educational path was definitely not Ivy League (University of Florida, where he played basketball).

Bill flawlessly executed his plan from where he was to where he wanted to be. Following college, Bill came back to his home state of Texas to work as an engineer for Compaq computer and a technical marketer for AMD's embedded processor division.

As a classic example of Breaking In, Gurley used his MBA at UT McCombs to transition his career from engineering to investing. This is a common path to Wall Street: spend 2-3 years working in an industry to gain knowledge and contacts, then complete your MBA at a school where top Wall Street firms recruit and get a job analyzing the companies you used to work for.

Gurley spent his first 3 years on Wall Street at Credit Suisse where we met. He was the lead analyst discussing the prospects for computer companies' stock prices. He had great stock recommendations and was often the #1 ranked analyst in the world for his stock picks, but I could tell when we met, this was only a pit-stop in his career.

Gurley was headed to VC. That was his end destination. The big problem was PCs and computers were mature, so there wasn't any active Venture Capital investment in the industry where Gurley had built his career.

Deutsche Bank (DB) provided the opportunity for Gurley to pivot. It was the crazy go-go days of the late '90s internet. DB was building a team of top analysts in the US as part of their effort to capitalize on the big fees all the other banks were earning by taking internet companies public. They wanted Gurley. He was already at a top bank. So, he said he would join DB but not as their PC/Computer analyst. He'd join as their internet analyst. DB agreed. Gurley went on to be the internet analyst at DB, taking Amazon public. He was then seen as the internet platform guy.

Companies like to hire what they know, i.e., they have already seen you be successful at something, so they hire you to do that same thing for them. Transitions like the one Gurley pulled off are not impossible but are easier done in an environment of rapid change where there are no experts in the new area and the ability to hire someone else is low.

In the late 1990s, the internet was so new there were no experienced analysts. It was a level playing field and a perfect time for Gurley to join. Look to take advantage of these industry transitions in your career too.

Gurley's ultimate destination was Venture Capital, and the transition he pulled off in investment banking made sure that he was in a vibrant sector of VC. He first joined Hummer Winblad Venture Partners as a partner, and shortly after, Gurley joined Benchmark, where for over 20 years he has focused on internet platform investments such as Uber. Gurley's net worth is estimated at more than $8 billion.

Lessons: (1) The most critical wealth step is your move from Breaking In to Building Equity and doing it at the right time. (2) Having a plan and knowing where you are going increases your likelihood of success. (3) You do not need to found a startup to build $100 million or even billions in wealth.

Sheryl Sandberg - When 2nd is Winning

You may be reading this knowing you don't see yourself as a founder, CEO, or venture investor. Sheryl Sandberg is a billionaire ($1.8 billion according to Forbes), yet hasn't been the big boss either.

She was able to build an impressive early career track record, spot a winner, and negotiate hard for her equity. I have been in the #2 slot as COO in a startup, and I can tell you that simply getting the COO role isn't enough to make billions.

Your wealth generation from startup equity depends on the prospects of the company, phase of the startup, and how much equity you negotiate for as part of your pay package.

Sandberg took one of the classic starts to top careers: management consulting. After growing up in Washington DC, Sheryl Sandberg received her BA (1991) and MBA (1995) from Harvard with the highest academic distinction and joined McKinsey & Company as a management consultant for a year. Going back to her DC roots, from 1996 to 2001, she was Chief of Staff to the then United States Secretary of the Treasury Larry Summers until Summers left to return to Harvard as its 27th president.

In 2001, Sandberg became the vice president of Global Online Sales & Operations for Google, Inc. Sandberg was in charge of the development of AdWords and AdSense, both of which helped Google become a profitable company. This track record helped her gain notoriety among VCs who knew Mark Zuckerberg needed a strong #2 for his hypergrowth unprofitable private company, Facebook.

In 2007, Sandberg met Mark Zuckerberg, the founder of Facebook, at a Christmas party and through several other meetings arranged by interested VCs. They met frequently to see if it was a good psychological and cultural fit. According to the New Yorker, by February of 2008, Zuckerberg had concluded that Sandberg would be perfect. "There are people who are really good managers, people who can manage a big organization," he says, "and then there are people who are very analytic or focused on strategy. Those two types don't usually tend to be in the same person. I would put myself much more in the latter camp." - Mark Zuckerberg.

Four years later, Facebook went public. Sandberg had negotiated for a large enough share of equity that she became a billionaire as a strong #2 in a very valuable company.

Typically, COOs can garner 5-10% of the equity of a seed stage startup, but by the time these startups have raised A, B, C, D, E, and more rounds, their equity percentage has diluted significantly. One solution is to negotiate hard for a larger share earlier as Sandberg did. Another is to become known as a person who can successfully prepare for and lead a company through a hot IPO. That's our next case study.

Lessons: (1) You do not have to start a company or lead a company in order to generate more than $100 million in wealth. (2) Don't assume. Ask. Originally, Zuckerberg thought Sheryl Sandberg would never be interested in working at "tiny" Facebook when she was at the giant Google. (3) Networking is critical so that people know your accomplishments and consider introducing you to the best opportunities.

Frank Slootman - IPO Billionaire

You may be reading these case studies thinking that you don't have the stomach to spend decades in the wild and wooly startup world. You may prefer larger, more stable companies. These larger, private companies can be part of your MegaWealth path.

I first met Frank Slootman when he was taking Service Now public as its CEO. He has since done the same with Snowflake, personally earning a cool billion dollars in equity value increase on the IPO day alone. He has written a book called *Amp it Up.* That says it all.

Slootman is a no-nonsense brilliant man. We may glamorize startups, but any VC-funded startup is expected to grow fast, as they need to generate returns for their investors. After years of this, employees and management experience burnout. Perhaps they are the right people for the early phases of the company but not the right people to lead a public company.

Every year, these startups need to show growth, a.k.a. "traction," that is as good as or better than the year before so they can raise more money at a higher valuation. (Otherwise, the equity of the founders will be diluted so much that they will have no reason to work at their own startup anymore.) Often, just when they are preparing for an IPO, the firmwide energy is at max burnout.

Slootman comes in and "Amps it Up" by bringing in his own high energy team, especially next level salespeople, while letting go of those who are not moving fast enough. This results in a reinvigoration of the company and its growth rate. This then leads to an attractive IPO valuation, driving up the returns for VC investors.

The downside? Getting the highest growth and valuation at the IPO date can lead to some digestion afterwards (sideways to down stock prices as well as tough growth numbers to try and improve for the following year). Slootman optimizes for a specific outcome: maximum IPO price. After a period of post-IPO digestion, his companies have had great success, especially Service Now, which dominates its market.

Lessons: (1) You do not need to spend years slugging it out and betting on startups where 90% of early stage companies fail. (2) Pay attention to your personality. Where will your skills be rewarded financially? (3) Becoming known for making other people money doing one narrow thing can make you billions.

Meg Whitman - Later Still Works

I was seated next to Meg at a Goldman Sachs conference in June 1998. She had just joined eBay in March of that year when they had 30 employees and revenues of approximately $4 million. Coming from a history of working in mega consumer brands, she was a very unlikely choice to run an internet company.

She took the Ivy route as a Princeton undergrad and a Harvard MBA. Like Sheryl Sandberg, Whitman spent years as a management consultant. She started as a brand manager at Procter & Gamble and later spent close to a decade in management consulting at Bain & Co. Her next decade was spent at Walt Disney Company, Stride Rite Corporation, and Florists' Transworld Delivery where she was CEO in 1995. In 1997, Meg was head of Hasbro's Playskool division, overseeing two children's brands: Playskool and Mr. Potato Head. She also imported the UK's children's television show Teletubbies into the U.S.

Meg Whitman spent two decades in the Breaking In phase, but her move to eBay in 1998 catapulted her into the $100 millionaire club and beyond.

Lessons: (1) Don't eliminate yourself from lucrative roles because you aren't the obvious choice or you think it's too late for you. (2) Keep an eye out for non sequitur career moves at key moments in new technologies. (3) Some companies and industries have so much wind at their backs you don't need to be the most knowledgeable or the most prepared in order to have great financial success.

And...

What are the biggest lessons I have learned in my time working for five billionaires and being exposed to many other wealthy individuals?

There are many ways to make money, so don't get discouraged when I use billionaires as examples. Most of these billionaires started from zero. Many of my former mentees who are now millionaires couldn't afford state college. My friends who made $100 million by age 50 started with nothing. Each of them took different paths to millions, but these paths share common traits.

My frameworks take the commonalities I have seen to give you the highest chance for success.

What to Expect from Implementing Your Money Flywheel

You've seen examples of the money flywheel in action, including how many different ways there are to win with your money flywheel activated. So, what can you expect from implementing it yourself?

By designing your money flywheel (your end destination) and knowing where you are in the 3Bs Framework (your map), like Bill Gurley, you'll know where you're going and how to get there. Having an end destination and a map will impact you every day as it does for many of my clients. With each phone call, networking opportunity, or business meeting, you'll know what to say 'yes' to, and more importantly, what to say 'no' to. You'll be moving forward towards your goals every single day.

You'll build moonshot goals for your career and wealth with achievable milestones to celebrate. Too many people I speak with don't dream big enough. Not dreaming big enough leads to reaching your goals too soon and feeling unmotivated to push for more.

Instead, build big, huge, moonshot goals. To feel regular accomplishment and encouragement, create achievable milestones along the way. Celebrate your milestones without minimizing your big goals.

Over the short term, we overestimate our capabilities, but over the long term, we underestimate ourselves. Why? Compounding. Our skills, knowledge, network, and wealth all benefit from compounding, but it's hard for our brains to grasp the amazing growth that can result.

You'll align your values, personality, and life with your path to have sustainably high energy and motivation to reach your goals. Often, when I start coaching someone, I bring up values and they brush it off, saying they only want to talk about their career. Values and value alignment with your personality traits drive your sense of purpose, which is your greatest life force.

Identifying and aligning your values with your destination will make your journey more fun and also more achievable.

You'll understand and navigate your most effective pathways to wealth by designing your own money flywheel and timing your move to Building Equity using the 3Bs Framework.

As you saw from the case studies, there are many ways to generate significant wealth. Some involve luck. All involve timing, but not all paths will be right for you. Moving into Building Equity and designing your Money Flywheel is effective because you stand in your value. You get paid equity, not just salary, for the value that you create.

You'll optimize your strategy and timing of moves, from Breaking In, to Building Equity, to Breaking Out. The biggest issue is often timing. How to stay in the Breaking In phase long enough, but not too long. This book will help you figure out the optimal timing and strategy for making those important transitions in your career and wealth.

Beyond the timing, how do you design your personal Money Flywheel, including selecting the right industry, the right company, and the right moment in your career to make your move? Using my 25 years as an industry analyst on Wall Street, managing billions, and working for 5 billionaires, I share my top ways to strategize your career as you would your biggest investment ever. You'll have frameworks to decide when, where, and how to make your moves in your path to MegaWealth.

CHAPTER 2: WHO THIS BOOK IS FOR

My knowledge centers around the technology industry, but the lessons can be applied to any healthy growing industry. There are many paths to MegaWealth. I share my firsthand knowledge of what can generate $100 million or more in wealth if navigated correctly: startups, venture capital, board directors, private equity, and hedge funds. The industries that feed into those paths are investment banking, management consulting, and more generally large technology companies (or large companies in an industry that has a vibrant startup ecosystem).

You may be in investment banking, management consulting, a big tech company, or in some related knowledge-based industry. This book will give you the biggest benefit when you are thinking about moving from Breaking In to Building Equity and want to do so in a way that maximizes your wealth.

Often, I am asked, "Are you worth $100 million?" Fair question. The answer is not yet. What qualifies me to write these books on making $100 million? I have worked for 5 billionaires, witnessed 2 close friends make $100 million (starting with nothing) by age 50, and coached multiple students (also starting with nothing) to become millionaires by age 30, well on their way to $100 million by age 50.

Why do I do this? Because I missed multiple onramps and don't want you to make the same mistakes. Here's a bit of my wealth story.

My Trade of a Lifetime

It was June of 2000. I was a partner at a top hedge fund, Palantir Capital. Markets were rocketing higher every day. One morning, I recommended we bet $2 billion that semiconductors would go *down*.

I was betting against everyone else.

I knew my billionaire boss had hired me to get this ONE trade right. I was as terrified as I was certain in my conviction. If you're too early, you lose hundreds of millions. Too late, you lose hundreds of millions.

One morning, I told my boss, "Everything in the semiconductor space is going down 80% from here. We should sell and go short."

He acted boldly, selling $1 billion in semis and shorting $1 billion for a $2 billion swing in under 2 weeks. My partners called me, yelling ... "You're crazy and will ruin Palantir!" Within days of our trade, semis started going down - and kept going down - declining 80% for a 5X return on our short.

My hedge fund boss personally made over $100 milion on that ONE trade.

The year before, I'd made my previous boss $24 million by running the #1 fund in the world. I saw what it takes to make big money, but I was still largely making money for other people, not myself.

Backing up a bit...

When I was 16, I started investing money I'd saved and earned, and by the time I was 20, through a string of luck (along with good advice and high risk), I turned $1,800 into $320,000. Then, I took a detour and became a horse trainer. My path had multiple detours.

When you look at billionaires and $100 millionaires, their paths might seem unattainable. Maybe mine seems that way to you. We can't see ourselves following the paths of billionaires like Bill Gates or Elon Musk because we only see their successes.

Both in my story and in those of my clients and other famous people, you'll see they did a lot right, but they also took more detours than you might think. You'll be surprised how much you can get wrong and still succeed if you get the big things (like your money flywheel) right.

Back to my path... I used grad school to change careers from horse trainer to institutional investor and get back on track.

After my MBA at USC, I worked for the billionaire "junk bond king" and pardoned felon Mike Milken. Milken taught me how to build wealth using leverage. I used what he taught me to accelerate my career, starting with working multiple roles at my next job.

At Farmers Insurance Investments, I simultaneously ran a $1B bond fund, a $300M energy fund, and a $350M tech fund as the most junior person there. Having multiple roles allowed me to build my experience in parallel and fast track that part of my career. Next, I joined Nicholas Applegate where I launched and co-ran the Nicholas | Applegate Global Tech Fund, which was up 630% in the first 12 months.

I made my billionaire boss $24M from his $4M investment, but I was only paid $135K that year. So, I left to join the top hedge fund, Palantir Capital, where I made my trade of a lifetime. What was next after my trade of a lifetime?

Here's where I went off track (again).

The logical next steps to my MegaWealth were launching my own fund or joining a tech startup in Silicon Valley. I had a phenomenal track record and hedge funds were popular, so I could have raised and run a large fund. Or, I could have gone to

Silicon Valley where tech stocks were dirt cheap in 2003 and made a fortune by joining a startup for equity.

Instead, I thought it would be fun to try out for the Olympics and take a year off. I have ridden horses since I was a kid. As I started my career, I figured that if I never stopped riding, I could be ready to take my riding to the next level when I had the time or funds to advance.

I made enough as an investor to buy some well trained horses. Based on my competition results, I was invited to compete on behalf of the US in Germany in 2004 during the Olympic trials and placed 9th in the US Trials for the World Cup team in 2005.

While it was fun, I decelerated my career. When I returned to Wall Street, I played it safe as an employee - not an owner. Why did I lose momentum? Was it the distraction of the horses?

I failed to moonshot my career goals. I didn't have a framework like the 3Bs, understand the potential of an activated money flywheel, or know how far I could go. I set my sights on achievements like working at a top hedge fund and being a well-respected investor. I beat those goals massively by running the #1 fund in the world in 1999 and then going to work as one of only 3 analysts for the best hedge fund of that era.

Once I surpassed my goals, I sat around wondering what was next. I had no map. No bigger plan.

My failing to have truly aspirational goals meant I could accomplish everything I set out to while staying in the Breaking In phase of my career. Not having big enough goals resulted in me taking another 14 years to make the move to Silicon Valley and the Building Equity phase.

My only wish is that I had been brave enough to make this transition 14 years earlier than I did.

My horse trainer, Hubertus Schmidt, who was 4th individually in the Athens Olympics, said it best, "*Warm up as much as necessary but as short as possible.*" This also holds true for the Breaking In phase of your career.

My years of riding and investing taught me you either move forward or backwards. Your bank balance is either going up or down. You only keep a horse in a certain phase as long as necessary, then you move them up. Competitive horses, like competitive people, don't like to stagnate.

I knew this from my years at Palantir Capital. Our trader would freak out if we ever were in the red. Yes, losing money sucks, but the real issue was psychological. Losing, stagnating, and moving backwards starts a phase of learned helplessness. Worse yet, you fall into sunk cost thinking and take more and more risk, overpaying to get back to where you were.

I knew in my bones that I was stagnating, even sliding backwards, undoing the hard work that I had put into the fast ascent of my early career.

Once I set my sights on it, with new goals, I made it to the next level, to the Building Equity phase. I became an advisor, operator, and, most importantly, OWNER.

What's life like now? What's it like to have made the transition to Building Equity and have my money flywheel fully operational?

I work with interesting people, advise startups, coach high-performing professionals, participate as a VC LP (limited partner), and build interesting businesses. I earn more while working less. Work feels fun because I interact with brilliant people on interesting problems. I prioritize my health, fitness, and friends.

The best part of my day is working with people to show them how to make this move to Building Equity earlier and more effectively than I did. I've found the same systems, frameworks, and philosophies that apply across many billionaires and $100 millionaires are effective for guiding the next generation to their MegaWealth paths.

These are people just like you who are driven to learn the strategic ways to build wealth the way those in Silicon Valley do. Their futures and your future are brighter for being proactive, but before you figure out where you want to go, take a second and check in with where you are now.

Self-Assessment: Are you stuck in the Breaking In phase of your career?

Rate yourself on a scale from 1 to 5 (1 = disagree, 5 = agree), then add up your total points.

1. I feel like I am part of the "Broke Upper Class" with nice cars, a nice house, and a nice life, yet feel that I'm on a treadmill at work, trying to earn more each year while my expenses seem to rise equally fast or faster.

2. I add far more value to the company I work at than I am paid.

3. I have friends and/or former co-workers who moved into ownership roles at companies and have made more money than I have, but they aren't as smart or hard-working as I am.

4. I have a great track record of proven accomplishments such that I could see myself being recruited for a leadership role at a private company.

5. I feel stagnant in my current role.

6. I have more to contribute from a leadership perspective, but there isn't room for me in leadership where I work.

7. I regret passing up opportunities to move to smaller, more dynamic companies where I could have earned equity.

8. I wonder what the right timing is, and if it's too late for the next phase in my career.

Sunriser (8-20 points)

You're fairly happy where you are and do not feel too frustrated or stagnant. Maybe you need a bit more time to build a good track record of accomplishments you can point to. Then, you can be paid what you are worth in equity at a high-quality private company. But, also consider if this comfort is because you prefer the "knowns" in life. Chapters 3, 5, and 10 can help you see the path to Building Equity, help you dive in deeper on getting your timing right, and help you determine if you are missing out before you wait too long like I did.

Sunsetter (21-40 points)

You're frustrated. It's likely beyond the time for you to move from Breaking In to Building Equity. You have accomplishments you can point to that will make you sought after by top firms. You'll be able to command your value in equity. Your friends have made the move. All you need to know is how to make the right move. Your career is your single biggest investment by far. Chapters 6 and 8 will go through the frameworks you'll use to build your career map and devise a plan to get there. Chapters 9, 10, and 11 will cover mindset factors, timing, and investing strategies needed to make your move.

If a successful billionaire like Peter Thiel regrets wasting time before moving from Breaking In to Building Equity, how can we mere mortals hope to do it right? Further, what is the biggest challenge I see knowledge workers wanting to become industry titans face?

Getting the move from Breaking In to Building Equity right requires:

1. Picking the right industry sector.
2. Joining the right company in that sector.
3. Pulling the trigger at the right time for that industry, for that company, and also for you in your career trajectory.

So, if you feel a bit overwhelmed after the self-assessment, know that you're in good company, including billionaires with regrets. Also, rest assured, this book will show you how to make those decisions.

CHAPTER 3: OVERCOMING YOUR BIGGEST HURDLES - COMMON PUSHBACKS TO BUILDING MEGAWEALTH

This book is for those who have been working at least 3-5 years in Big Tech with specific accomplishments they can point to, wondering when to make the move to Building Equity, likely in a private company.

This book is also for those who followed the early career paths of investment banking or management consulting and want a map for moving into the Building Equity phase of their careers.

This book is for those working as knowledge workers for a salary, feeling more and more a part of the Broke Upper Class. You work in an industry that has a growing private company ecosystem, and you want to understand how to pick the right company and industry in order to move to the Building Equity phase of your career.

What if you are earlier or later than those I mentioned above? This book will meet you where you are on your path to wealth. Whether you are Breaking In, wondering when to make the move to Building Equity, or are already Building Equity in the startup world but want to strategically architect your career to create the most wealth, this book can help you go from reactionary mode to being in control of your destiny.

Do you think the Broke Upper Class is full of people trying to get by on $75,000? I know successful bulge bracket investment bankers who make millions working 80-hour weeks but have no control over their calendars. In order to appease their families for their absence, they have multiple houses, fancy vacations, and more, and there never seems to be enough money. That's the Broke Upper Class!

No matter if you are only a few years into your career or are more established, as long as you are selling your time for money, you are destined to be part of the Broke Upper Class. The answer is to separate your time spent from your money earned via Building Equity and activating your money flywheel, which allows for step-function increases in your wealth.

The biggest challenge for you will be timing your move to make your time in Breaking In as short as possible but as long as necessary.

You just took the self-assessment. Write down your thoughts on your answers as well as whether you agree with the results. You may be feeling resistance, feeling like it can't be that simple. (It is simple...but not easy.)

Here are some common pushbacks I hear.

Don't you need money to make money?

Let's do a quick self-assessment. Rate how much you agree with the following 3 questions or statements (1 = disagree, 5 = agree), then add up your score.

1. The only people I know who have money started with money and invested it to grow their wealth.
2. When someone starts with a little money, they get stuck in a loop of living from paycheck to paycheck, so it's difficult to build a nest egg.

3. People who say you can make big money starting from nothing are lying.

Open to possibilities (3-6)

Even if you are starting with very little, you have seen others start from nothing and make it big. You think you can too if you have the right tools, put in the effort, and build your knowledge. Building your money flywheel (Chapters 4, 6, 8, and 12) and investing skills (Chapter 11) will help you make your belief a reality!

Still Skeptical (7-15)

You don't believe you can make money without starting with money. While I understand this skepticism, especially if you haven't seen success stories firsthand, the first step for you is internalizing some of the stories throughout this book. Allow yourself to think success is possible. Chapter 9 about having a MegaWealth Mindset can help.

Some of those I have guided couldn't afford state college. Greg Magadini paid his way through community college as an amateur boxer. First, starting from nothing, he founded the UCSD trading community and traded stocks while in college, and from that got a job at a trading firm. That trading firm was purchased by a larger one. The larger firm traded cryptocurrencies among other assets.

Between his new firm and the other connections he had, Greg made hundreds of thousands trading in cryptocurrency. Then he bought real estate with the proceeds. Next, he had a chance to co-found a cryptocurrency options analytics software company, which he later sold.

Money compounds over time. Starting earlier gave him more time to compound the money from his early wins. The fact that Greg's "exit" - i.e. his profits from selling his company, was early (before the age of 32) means he has time to compound his millions for decades to come. He's on his way to $100 million.

The founder of KFC was worth $3 million when he died. KFC was a big idea, but it started hitting on all cylinders when he was 60. He simply didn't have enough time to compound his money.

This is why I've historically wanted my mentees to have made $3-$10 million by age 30 and compound from there. Marc Andreessen did the same. If you are over 30 and don't have millions, don't despair! Meg Whitman was in her 40s when she got the eBay role and still reached billionaire status. Getting those early wins increases your likelihood of reaching your goals, but that doesn't mean it isn't possible with a later start.

Mini-Exercise: Now that you've seen your self-assessment score on needing money to make money and you've read my thoughts on the matter, write down a sentence or two about where you stand (agree/disagree) on whether this pushback will truly hold you back.

I don't know anyone. I don't have a network.

Let's do a quick self-assessment. Rate how much you agree with the following 3 questions or statements (1 = disagree, 5 = agree), then add up your score.

1. The people I do know, my friends and family, aren't in any influential positions in high-leverage careers.
2. I don't know how to build a new network from scratch. Where will I start?
3. I don't like networking, especially when I am meeting brand new people who can impact my career. It's stressful.

Charismatic Connector (3-6)

Congrats! You are a natural connector. You can see the potential in every connection you have and are also confident you can build the network you need. If any of your scores are below where you'd like, I recommend you read Chapter 9, the connected mind, and Chapter 7 on picking the right industry and company to target.

Solo Flyer (7-15)

Many people get stressed over networking and thus avoid it. If this is you, try these tips. Less is more in networking. Talk less, ask more, and let the other person do all the talking and work. They'll like you more when they are talking.

To build the network you need, follow these 3 steps:

1. Know whom you want to meet. Analyze the industry, companies, and players (Chapter 7).
2. Build your personal CRM, including those you want to meet (Chapters 8 and 13).
3. Use techniques in the Connected Mind (Chapter 9) to build strong relationships.

There are two possible issues with not having a network. First, you haven't mapped out your path to wealth and therefore you don't know who you should network with. This book shows you the paths and how to execute on them. Know your path and you'll know where to focus your networking.

The second issue is having the wrong network for the goals you have in mind. Once you know your path, you may look at the people you know and realize they aren't going to help get you where you want to go. You'll need to build a new network!

This book (Chapter 9, The Connected Mindset) covers how to build human connections and amplify your networking skills.

Then, we dive deeper into how to choose the industries and companies to target (Chapter 7) and the investors in those industries and companies (Chapter 11).

Network into these industries, companies, and investors to achieve your career and wealth goals. Build the network which will support your efforts of Building Equity in a sector with leverage and upside potential.

This book shows you how to build the right network for your goals.

Mini-Exercise: Now that you've seen your self-assessment score on perhaps not having the right network or worrying about building one and you've read my thoughts on the matter, write down a sentence or two about where you stand (agree/disagree) on whether this pushback will truly hold you back.

I worry about making the wrong moves.

Let's do a quick self-assessment. Rate how much you agree with the following 3 questions or statements (1 = disagree, 5 = agree), then add up your score.

1. You have seen your friends go from job to job, often for shorter periods (9-18 months), with no clear career direction. It seems people choose their next move based on incoming offers. There has to be a better way.

2. It seems like people who made the right career moves only figured out after the fact that their moves were genius. They were simply lucky.

3. You have friends who jumped into a small company too fast and were relegated to working for small, underfunded companies. Worse, they were unable to break back into more established companies.

Ready to Leap (3-6)

You have seen the bad moves but know that, while this can happen, the chances of it happening to you are greatly reduced because you are reading this book and taking steps to think about building your wealth and career strategically. Chapter 8 will give you perspective on how to design your destination, your money flywheel, and where you are in the 3Bs Framework. Chapters 7, 10, and 11 will help you to optimize the direction and timing of your move.

Frozen with Fear (7-15)

It is already stressful enough thinking about moving from a comfortable, salaried position with a clear career path to betting on yourself and joining a fast-moving startup (at any phase, early or late). There are so many factors. Did you choose the right industry and company at the right time for that industry and company and at the right time for your career? Yes, there is a bit of luck involved, but mapping out your plan while removing roadblocks to success can greatly improve your chances while reducing your anxiety. Chapter 8 shows you the step-by-step process to building your MegaWealth Plan, from designing your flywheel, to knowing where you are in the 3Bs, to removing roadblocks, and finally building your plan.

Mini-Exercise: Now that you've seen your self-assessment score on the risk of making the wrong moves and you've read my thoughts on the matter, write down a sentence or two about where you stand (agree/disagree) on whether this pushback will truly hold you back.

This book gives you frameworks and research to be able to analyze your moves and build the best strategic approach to your wealth and career. Of course, at any time, if you feel you need more of a personalized approach, individualized coaching is available. If you are interested, grab a 15 minute slot to talk.

I am not sure I am right for the startup world.

Let's do a quick self-assessment. Rate the following 3 statements (1 = disagree, 5 = agree), then add up your score.

1. Startups are the wild west. 90% of them fail. They have no structure, no idea who's doing what, and are stressful places to work.
2. Working at a startup is too risky if you have a family to support.
3. I am not one of those entrepreneurial people who started having ideas and selling things while still in high school or even grade school. My first job was at a real company.

True Blue Entrepreneur (3-6)

Entrepreneurship runs through your veins. Since you were young, you thought up clever ways to make money and sell things. Now that you're older, working at a startup doesn't scare you. It excites you. However, this doesn't necessarily mean you should focus on super tiny companies. Think about the stories I have shared so far - some started their own companies and some learned the ropes at larger companies first, then joined a later-stage private company. See Chapters 7, 11, and 12 for choosing the right company, industry, stage, and timing as well as how to look at your career like an investment.

Startup Skeptic (7-15)

You know the stats. You may have seen friends waste years of time and money on startups that went to zero. Your career has been corporate, but you're starting to feel like part of the Broke Upper Class. You wonder if there is a way to move out of the Breaking In phase in corporate and into Building Equity in private companies without taking on the 90% failure risk of early stage startups.

Startups are not all the same. Many are large and still growing yet more stable than those in their first years. As I shared in Chapter 1, some executives like Frank Slootman, CEO of Snowflake, became billionaires by entering a startup 18 months before IPO and leading them through the IPO.

If you are more familiar with public companies and public equities, I strongly urge you to open your mind to private markets. It is not all 2-person startups working out of their parents' garages (Apple Computer). In fact, private equity companies like Thoma Bravo only invest in companies with minimum annual revenues of $1 billion. According to Forbes, 86% of the largest (500+ employees) US companies are private, not public.

Mini-Exercise: Now that you've seen your self-assessment score on whether you are built for the startup world and you've read my thoughts on the matter, write down a sentence or two about where you stand (agree/disagree) on whether this pushback will truly hold you back.

I don't know anything about private equity or venture capital.

Let's do a quick self-assessment. Rate how much you agree with the following 3 questions or statements (1 = disagree, 5 = agree), then add up your score.

1. Private equity is only for those who get into a top investment bank and are then recruited into top PE firms, like Blackstone or Apollo.

2. If I missed the early onramp, private equity isn't possible for me.

3. Private equity requires the same deal-making skills as investment banks. Since I didn't start at an investment bank, private equity isn't an option for me.

Big World Thinker (3-6)

You are open to private markets, even if you don't know where to start. You have a feeling that both private equity and private markets can be target-rich. This book will show you how to network into private equity opportunities. Your only job right now is to keep an open mind.

Privately Unsure (7-15)

You are not sure private equity is for you. It seems to be for people who knew the route early, from going Ivy League, to investment banking at a top firm, to getting recruited into PE. While this is one route, there are many more. You'll go from feeling skeptical to excited at the sheer volume of opportunities you didn't know existed!

Mini-Exercise: Now that you've seen your self-assessment score on perhaps not knowing anything about private equity or venture capital and you've read my thoughts on the matter, write down a sentence or two about where you stand (agree/disagree) on whether this pushback will truly hold you back.

I don't want to work that hard.

Let's do a quick self-assessment. Rate how much you agree with the following 3 questions or statements (1 = disagree, 5 = agree), then add up your score.

1. Life balance and family time is more important to me than being wealthy. No company or career can have my weekends!

2. People focus too much on achievement and money. Real wealth is not needing to work because your expenses are low (minimalist lifestyle).

3. Work is what I do to pay for my weekends and vacations. I will not grind away, work long hours, or work weekends.

Prepare for Liftoff (3-11)

This book is for those who want to work hard for massive rewards. You've already built the work ethic and stamina by putting in long hours. You're here to make sure those hours are spent wisely - on activities that will give you the highest returns for your efforts. You may want to check out Chapters 7 and 10 on picking the best company and industry, timing your move, and how to use your valuable time to move towards your MegaWealth goal.

Dismount! (12-15)

If you want all your weekends off and life balance from day one, then this book is not for you. If you think achievement is overrated, consider gifting this book to one of your overachiever friends. However, if you scored closer to 12 and want to continue with this book, check out Chapter 9 on MegaWealth Mindsets and Chapter 13 for your personal values audit. Be honest with yourself if this is who you want to be and what you want to do.

Pro tip: Those who make millions don't work *that* much harder than those on a regular salary toiling away on the treadmill of trying to keep their incomes growing faster than their expenses (the "Broke Upper Class").

What if your values and purpose aligned with a wealth path that requires hard work but separates your time from wealth such that, by your 50s or 60s, you could have far more wealth yet work less than your peers (and work on things you find interesting)?

Mini-Exercise: Now that you've seen your self-assessment score on perhaps not wanting to work that hard, and you've read my thoughts on the matter, write down a sentence or two about where you stand (agree/disagree) on whether this pushback will truly hold you back.

The Biggest Overall Hurdle?

The one I struggled with the most? Making the move from Breaking In to Building Equity while seeding your MegaWealth Money Flywheel with foresight, research, and confidence.

We are all busy. We go to work each day not stepping back and deciding where we are going long term. The 3Bs Framework gives you that perspective. The framework is a proven method to pause, step back, and map your career path to separating your wealth creation from your time.

What is the key to unlocking the value of the 3Bs Framework? Building your money flywheel as you transition from Breaking In to Building Equity. In the next chapter, I reveal why nearly all $100 millionaires have active money flywheels and why you need one too.

CHAPTER 4: THE SECRET KEY TO MEGAWEALTH

The secret key to massively increasing your likelihood of success in moving from Breaking In to Building Equity is to build your money flywheel (your simultaneous roles as a builder, investor, and advisor). Your money flywheel will naturally occur as you navigate the Building Equity phase of the 3Bs Framework.

I call it a money flywheel because not only do each of the 3 roles give you multiple chances at step-function increases in wealth through liquidity events but when you design a life that includes all three roles, the *interaction between the roles* increases your opportunity for wealth building. Sound too good to be true? Don't worry, I'll share stories and examples of how this happens throughout the book.

The flywheel effect happens when small wins build on each other over time and eventually gain so much momentum that growth almost seems to happen by itself – similar to the momentum created by a flywheel on a rowing machine.

Why build a money flywheel? Because it massively increases your surface area of opportunity. How?

One day, someone reached out to me on LinkedIn wanting "20 minutes" to discuss his career. He said he enjoyed my posts. I asked if he'd read my book. He bought it immediately. Three days later he messaged me that it all made sense and he knew what to do.

Three weeks after that, he made the transition from a leading sales role at a big tech firm (Breaking In) to a sales leadership role where he was paid in stock options plus salary at a fast-growing startup (Building Equity). He thanked me for writing the book.

A month after taking his new role, he messaged me wanting to talk. While he had successfully transitioned into Building Equity, he wanted a detailed plan. We worked together to create his MegaWealth Plan, which included, at the core, his MegaWealth Money Flywheel.

Now, several times a week, he messages me with wins. His company's CEO, VCs, and board are recognizing the strategic nature of his contributions. One of his target VC firms is considering him for an advisory position with the VC as well as board roles with their portfolio companies. He is an LP for a different VC firm and makes angel investments.

He knows what he wants his money flywheel, and broader career path, to look like. Now, he can prioritize conversations that will get him where he wants to go. He feels forward progress every day.

Creating a money flywheel is the most powerful action you can take to ensure your move from Breaking In to Building Equity yields maximum results.

What is a Money Flywheel?

Here's your first glimpse into the engine that drives big wealth. The money flywheel is the Silicon Valley Secret.

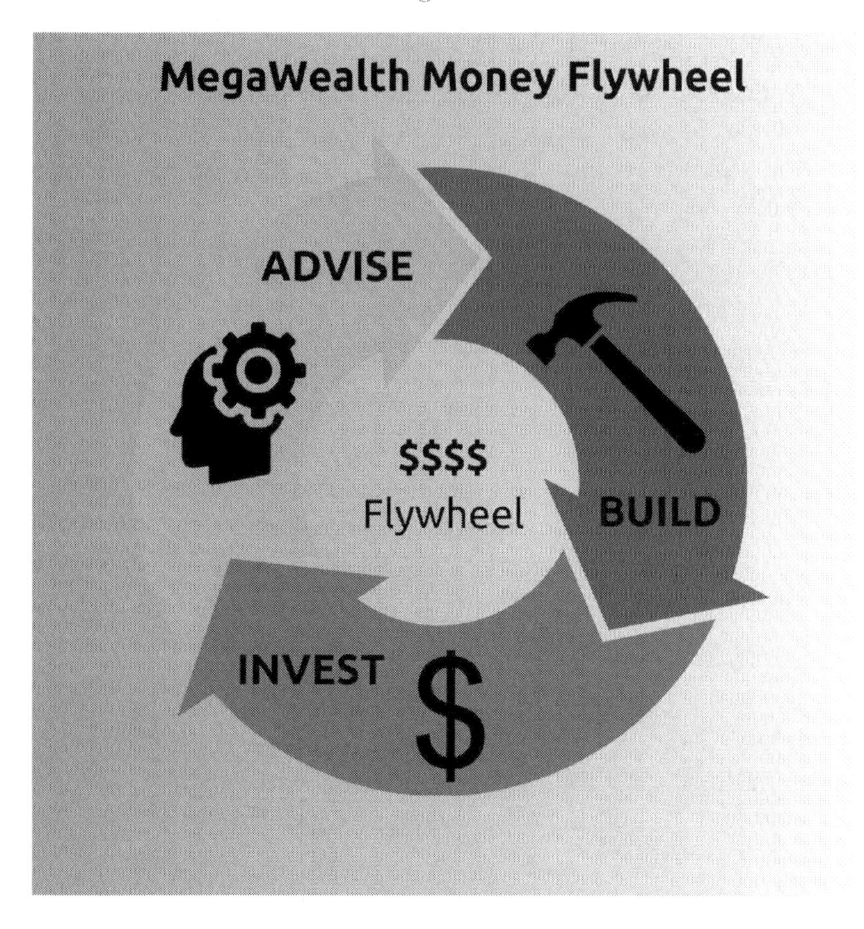

Build

The 3Bs Framework allows you to clearly see and plan for your move into Building Equity, the stage at which you seed your money flywheel. Being a key figure building a vibrant private company will get you noticed by that company's investors, i.e., Venture Capital (VC) and Private Equity (PE) firms. These investors will notice the positive impact your leadership is having on the growth of this private company. This will lead them to recommend you for board roles, other leadership roles at different private companies they are invested in, and later, once you have helped several of their portfolio companies, a part-time partner role at that VC or PE firm.

Invest

Investing is more than buying mutual funds, ETFs, or even public stocks. In the MegaWealth Money Flywheel, Invest is another way you'll participate in the private markets space. It is both a networking tool and a wealth building tool. As you rack up achievements and become more influential in the private company universe you've chosen, you'll build relationships with private investors (VC and/or PE firms). You may join them as a scout, advisor, or part-time partner, earning carry for your wisdom while still having your day job in your Build role.

Advise

As you execute in your Build role, other private companies wanting to follow that same trajectory will invite you to be on their boards of directors. This may start with you joining boards of advisors and later grow into board of directors' roles. These advisory groups and your VC/PE relationships are where you'll hear about your most lucrative and interesting next Build roles.

You might be thinking, "Wow! That money flywheel looks like 3 jobs!"

In fact, with multiple board roles, it can feel like more. But you'll find leverage everywhere. You'll learn things and network with people in each role that helps you in your other roles.

You'll be executing the Building Equity phase of the 3Bs Framework on multiple fronts at once. You'll have multiple at bats with potential home runs. Creating your money flywheel when you move into the Building Equity phase of the 3Bs Framework will supercharge your wealth building capacity.

A Day in The Life with Your Money Flywheel.

While ramping sales in your Build role, you will get noticed by VCs who will recommend you for board roles. Companies want you on their boards because you can help guide them to grow in the same way you did in your Build role. While on those boards, other board members may also be on boards of other companies. When they are searching for a new CEO, you may be at the top of their list. All this activity impresses the VCs you are advising, and they too will offer you more opportunities to advise for more equity.

Later, in Chapters 6 and 8, I go through, in detail, how to build your money flywheel. Here, I just want to give you a taste of the endless possibilities once you build one.

If building your money flywheel still seems like a crazy idea, here are a few real-life examples of people I have coached as well as friends I have gone through my career with who thrived with their money flywheels activated.

Money Flywheels in Action

Linda Xie - Build Your Money Flywheel Early.

I mentored Linda Xie when she was still in college. She researched Bitcoin for a college project and initially dismissed it as something only the criminals used. She started her career (Breaking In) at AIG (their financial arm) and later turned down an offer from Merrill Lynch when I advised her to stay at each position at least 3 years to show companies a track record of reliability.

While my view of this 3-year minimum per job is often questioned, I stand by this advice because of the economics. Quality companies invest time and resources in new hires, which often take 9-12 months to get up to speed. Then, companies start earning their investment back, and at the same time, employees start to hit their stride and rack up accomplishments in the second and third years. Exceptions exist, but this is my general thinking.

Linda used the Merrill offer to double her pay at AIG. Meanwhile, she had been conversing with classmates on the emergence of cryptocurrencies beyond Bitcoin. 3 years and 2 months after joining AIG, she accepted an offer to be one of the early employees (focused on compliance) at Coinbase. There, she built an incredible network of connections in crypto and became broadly known as a savvy operator and investor.

At age 27, Linda formed Scalar Capital with Jordan Clifford (also from Coinbase). She co-ran Scalar for 6 years. In classic Silicon Valley fashion, the founders of Coinbase were not angry that Linda left. They invested in her fund. This collaborative approach to investing later in talent you discover is central to many Silicon Valley entrepreneurs' money flywheels.

Linda is a great example of how you can move into the Building Equity phase early, build your money flywheel, and then move back and forth among your three flywheel roles. For 3 years, she helped build Coinbase while investing personally and advising several crypto projects. Then, she founded her own hedge fund, focusing more on investing and advising and less on building. Through that experience, she met more amazing builders, and now she is focused less on investing, more on advising, and is building a new startup.

Lessons: (1) The "Why" of your money flywheel is to follow your values, skills, and purpose while making money through your bigger surface area of opportunity. (2) You don't have to have one third of your time and effort in each bucket: build, invest, and advise. Have something in each bucket so that you can focus on what is working and double down on your efforts there. (3) Don't be afraid to follow your energy and instincts while respecting some basic rules of economics.

It may seem easier to see yourself by looking at those who aren't so far ahead, i.e., the billionaire examples may seem unreachable. I've coached people who are building their money flywheels. Friends of mine that you haven't heard of (I have changed their names to preserve their privacy) have quietly made $100 million by age 50. Here are my friends' stories.

Jenny Mathers, MD - From Builder to Board Director

My friend Jenny Mathers, MD, founded and/or helped build two unicorns before the age of fifty. She's proof that you can build your money flywheel through any path that includes high leverage careers. Jenny went to medical school and was practicing as a clinician and researcher. She started as a doctor and still is, but then she got drawn into biotech.

Even though her path started as a doctor, her journey to the Builder role of founder and C-suite followed one of the more traditional paths: first, management consulting to work with top companies, learn, and network; then, working at larger companies in the industry to further build her network; then, joining a promising startup in the C-suite.

After practicing as a physician, Jenny joined a top management consulting firm as a consultant in their healthcare practice. She focused her career on the immune system. After management consulting, Jenny spent six years at a top biotech firm as a medical director.

You'd think after working at a top biotech firm Jenny would be perfectly positioned to jump into the biotech startup world. Instead of jumping into a biotech startup, she went big, mega big, with her next step as a VP at one of the largest pharma companies in the world. What did she do for them? She introduced new drugs to the FDA on behalf of the company.

In this role, she got major attention and power as she brought new drugs through the FDA on behalf of one of the largest and most respected pharmaceutical companies in the world. She did it in her chosen specialty, which she focused on for the rest of her career. Jenny was the youngest person at a top pharma company filing new drugs with the FDA, once again proving you don't have to wait your turn.

After three years at this top pharma company, she joined the founding team of a small, private biotech firm as the Chief Medical Officer. In that role, she chose which illnesses to try and cure and what drugs had the most promise to cure them.

Then, she introduced these drugs to the FDA, where she had already built up trust and connections. Her biotech company went public via IPO, hit unicorn status, and sold for billions of dollars only a few years after going public. This is how you build $100 million careers . . . slowly at first, then all at once.

Lessons: (1) Your path can be unique to you but must be in industries that share certain characteristics. Learn more about choosing promising industries in Chapters 7 and 11. (2) You can skip steps, but often, the fastest route is not directly from management consulting to startups. Take the time to analyze which skills and connections you'll need, like Jenny did, and go build them. You may need to go big before going small. (3) Her money flywheel came *after* she hit $100 million. Everyone has a different path. Jenny built her money flywheel sequentially, focused on building exclusively until she hit 2 big exits, and now she has a fully operational money flywheel (she is on multiple boards, works as a part-time venture partner, and helps build other companies) because of her massive success in building.

Shelby - Skipping Over: From Investment Banker to Board Director

In the early 2000s, my friend, Shelby, a former investment banker, was going through her middle-age bucket list of adventures to complete before old age kicked in—mostly physical activities like running marathons, Ironmans, and bodybuilding. She also managed her own money. This, in effect, was her long-term plan after retiring early from Wall Street. Her investment banking career had generated enough wealth that as long as she kept compounding her wealth, she would never have to work again.

As she checked items off her bucket list and got some rest, she became bored. One day, we met for a walk, and she confided in me the harsh truth she hadn't expected.

"I've been pushing myself physically, but I miss competing with my mind," she said. "I want more."

Shelby explained how she wanted more intellectual stimulation because she still had a lot to share. She didn't need to work for the money anymore; she enjoyed the challenge and excitement of working with brilliant people.

Shortly after that conversation, she got a call from the CEO of a company she used to analyze when she was at the investment bank. The CEO asked what she was doing now and if she had ever considered board work. What made this amazing was that it's rare for financial analysts to get seats on boards of directors. Shelby had a solid background in mergers and had already demonstrated a deep understanding of the company, so the CEO called her.

Shelby's investment banking work had given her the opportunity to advise on several high-stakes deals in the past. She knew what it took to win and win big. Billions were on the line. This company's CEO knew this. He'd seen her in action and wanted that brilliance and advice on his board.

"Shelby, have you ever thought about a board seat?" he asked her.

"No, not really," she said

"Well . . . think it over," he said.

Shelby did. She thought it would be fascinating to learn about a company from a different perspective and see if her advice could prove useful. In the end, she joined, but it only lasted a few months because a larger competitor purchased the company. Having Shelby on the board with her investment banking background was useful during the merger negotiations.

While Shelby didn't get a seat on the larger company's board, a smaller, local tech company invited her on their board. She advised this company to switch from a hardware solution where they were competing with large, Asian manufacturers over to a software solution focused on serving a specific industry need. The rest of the board and company agreed. The strategy worked, and the stock price went up by twenty-five times with her options appreciating even more. This wasn't the only board she would serve on either. Over the next several decades, Shelby would build a second career that became more lucrative than the first one she retired from. She became a professional board director, being paid equity stakes for each of her board positions in multiple companies at once.

<u>Lessons</u>:(1) Whenever there is a rule, like you must start in investment banking and move into something else after 3 years, there is also an exception like Shelby. (2) Even with decades of board experience, Shelby tells me she cannot seek out board roles. Once offered the opportunity, then she can decide whether or not she wants to apply. (3) Your money flywheel can be very effective, as it is for Shelby (and Bill Gurley too), while excelling in just two of the three areas (Invest and Advise).

The real secret of building massive wealth is building a money flywheel. I share more on how to do this in Chapters 4, 6, 8, and 12. This is how most top players make big money in Silicon Valley and beyond. Elon Musk. Alexis Ohanian. Tim Ferriss. The list goes on.

Those who have built wealth using money flywheels also include my not-so-famous friends discussed above. This is how it's done. Each one has a different path, life, and work balance based on their skills and personality. You too can find your perfect balance.

Let's look at some of the more famous examples of money flywheels in full swing, keeping in mind many of these people started from zero.

Famous Money Flywheels

Elon Musk - Build and Reinvest in Your Money Flywheel

Elon Musk is famous for many things. He is ranked as one of the wealthiest people in the world. He is CEO of 3 companies (Tesla, SpaceX, and Twitter) at the same time, focusing his flywheel efforts squarely on Building. He also invests, not through being a partner in a traditional VC but as both an angel investor and by taking his early exits and putting all of those winnings into his next ventures.

Although he grew up in a wealthy family, by the time he was in college at Wharton, he was hosting ticketed parties to pay for his tuition. Elon has also been broadly interviewed about his issues reading people, his abusive childhood, and other emotional challenges he faces. You may not want to model your life after Elon's, but his money flywheel is another great example that no two are the same.

He builds big companies, chasing the dream of solving the world's hardest problems. In 1995, he founded Zip2 and sold it to Compaq in 1999, receiving $22 million for his share. He invested $12 million to found X.com that later merged into PayPal, which sold to eBay for $1.2 billion, netting Musk $176 million. That $176 million became his seed money for Tesla, SpaceX, the Boring Company, and more. Elon also invests in other projects. He was an early co-founder of Open AI, the creator of ChatGPT.

What about Elon's board of director roles? What he's thinking about and building combined with his investments keep him in the flow of what's new, next, and exciting. His board director roles seem to take a back seat, i.e., he has been a board chairman of a company he founded but does not go out seeking board positions. Given his wealth, connections, and companies he is building, he doesn't need to focus on getting board positions for wealth or for connections.

Lessons:(1) When finding your balance between Build/Invest/Advise in your money flywheel, focus on what you are good at. Elon is a Builder. For Musk, Invest and Advise play supporting roles. (2) You don't need to work as much or as hard as Elon does. (He is worth hundreds of *billions* of dollars, whereas this book covers how to reach $100 million.) (3) Building your money flywheel gives you the freedom to follow your passions and lean into your strengths.

Alexis Ohanian - Success without an "Exit"

Alexis is the founder of Reddit as well as a number of other startups, was a venture partner at Y Combinator, and founded two VC firms: Initialized Capital and SevenSevenSix. Alone, he is worth $150M in 2023, and he is also married to Serena Williams, whose net worth is $300M in 2023.

Alexis has executed the perfect money flywheel as a tech startup founder, VC partner, VC fund founder, and board director both through his VC investments and as a trusted advisor to other companies.

What is interesting here is that his biggest startup success is Reddit, and that hasn't sold or IPO'd. When we think about building wealth in startups, we often think in terms of exits (sale, merger, IPO). Alexis shows this is not the only route. Banks allow you to borrow against your equity stake in your company, or alternatively, you can sell shares of private companies in secondary markets. Secondary market sales of private shares are famously inefficient. You'll often receive a 25%-40% discount to fair market value for your shares. For this reason, most people use the lending route. Alexis can then take some money off the table to invest. His money flywheel is fully operational with wealth and opportunities generated from Build, Advise, and Invest.

Lessons: (1) For every "rule," there is an exception. (2) Your successful startup doesn't need to have a monetary exit for your money flywheel to work. (3) One of the benefits and keys to success is to follow your personality. Ohanian is a serial entrepreneur. Are you?

Tim Ferriss - Angel Aptitude

Just when you think you have the money flywheel mental model all figured out, I introduce a podcast host and bestselling author into the mix! As the stark opposite of Elon Musk's 3 CEO roles, Ferriss is famous for his books, *The 4-Hour Workweek* and *The 4-Hour Body*. He is all about efficiency in work. But, make no mistake: Tim Ferriss has a fully activated money flywheel.

Some have great timing, like Marc Andreessen entering the internet space in 1996 just before internet stocks rocketed straight up for 3 years. Ferriss had the timing of a survivor. In 2001, one year out of college, Ferris founded an e-commerce company during the depths of the dot-com bust. He sold this company to a private equity group.

Using the seed money from the sale of his first company and the connections he built, Tim Ferriss spent the next 15 years in Silicon Valley as a very successful angel investor and advisor, including getting pre-seed shares of Uber in return for being on their advisory board. While he did found a few other startups, Ferriss' massive success in his money flywheel was in the Invest and Advise spaces.

He also has a successful podcast along with a blog and multiple bestselling books. His podcast is a massive networking tool, allowing him to speak with the world's most interesting people, thus getting him more investment and advising opportunities.

Lessons: (1) Money flywheels are powerful because they are flexible. (2) Money flywheels are designed to allow you to express and capitalize off of your greatest gifts. (3) Analyzing other wealthy people's roles can help you see the power and choices available in building your own money flywheel.

Money Flywheel Self-Assessment:

Rate yourself on a scale from 1 to 5 (1 = disagree, 5 = agree).

I have multiple sources of *active* income (not passive income).

1. I know what roles I want in a private company that would maximize my money flywheel.
2. I have a plan to be a part-time venture partner, venture scouting partner, private equity scout, or technical advisor role.
3. I have a plan for how to join a board of directors.
4. I have more interesting opportunities being offered to me than I could ever handle.

Now, add up your total score from all the questions above.

Fly in the Ointment (5-12)

You may be thinking like a salaried worker, but all it takes to change is to see how a money flywheel can work for you! Chapters 6 and 8 will show you how to build your money flywheel and Chapter 9 will help you get in the right mindset to execute your money flywheel.

Ready to Fly (13-25)

You are starting to put in place the elements for your money flywheel. You know these elements are critical but may be missing some important details to flush out your individual plan. Chapters 6 and 7 will take you through the process so you go from great ideas to an exciting map of your future.

At first, the thought of building your own money flywheel may be overwhelming.

Whenever you wonder how you can accomplish all this, remember the following:

1. Most big successes started at zero. On average, inherited wealth is 90% depleted in three generations, so starting with money may not help.

2. Super wealthy, self-made people seem busy, but they have more calendar control and free time than regular, salaried workers. They also get to work on what interests them.

3. Many VCs are on 5-10 boards plus their normal day jobs as investors. For your flywheel, aim for 2-4 private company boards over time, remembering that private company boards take less of your time than large, public company boards.

4. Each of the three roles in your money flywheel will inform and help you do the other roles more efficiently.

Your money flywheel will be as unique as your career path, advising style and investing style. The key is to seed it early and often, knowing and leaning into your strengths as I know you can. To do this, you'll need to believe in yourself and take some risks as we'll discuss in the next chapter.

CHAPTER 5: THE CATCH - BIG OPPORTUNITIES REQUIRE GUTS

You may be wondering: if it's so simple to move from Breaking In to Building Equity, then build out your money flywheel, why doesn't everyone do it?

It's scary.

It's uncharted territory. It's not what your parents did.

The safest thing to do is to break into one career and stay there, in the Breaking In phase, for the rest of your career. That's where I was stuck for 14 years until I finally saw the light and got the nerve to make the move.

I too was stuck in the Breaking In phase.

I chose jobs based on what I liked to do day-to-day instead of how that role fit into the bigger picture of my career and my wealth. I enjoyed being an analyst and avoided portfolio management and client interactions because those weren't as fun for me.

This meant I didn't see that, as a portfolio manager, I could get a piece of the fund's performance, like equity in a company, and that would have separated my hours from my earnings in a step-function manner. I didn't see that interacting with clients might allow me to start my own fund after I built my track record.

When your wealth grows linearly, you earn 5% more a year in raises, or you earn 8% or even 10% average returns by investing in the S&P. Step-function increases in wealth come from liquidity events and exits, i.e., you have equity in a company either because you are in leadership at that company or are an investor or advisor. Then, that company goes through an IPO or sells and you earn 10X or 100X or more on what those shares were worth when you started.

What's the bottom line here? I could have been doing similar things (being an analyst, picking the right companies, advising companies on their strategic direction) while building equity, earning greater multiples of the money in equity for a similar amount of work. The same goes for you.

Don't miss the opportunity I initially missed.

I delayed my move to Building Equity and my money flywheel by 14 years. Once I made the move, I discovered I was able to build my wealth in a step-function way, doing similar and often more interesting work than I was doing before. That's why I designed the 3Bs Framework so you know how to optimally time your move into Building Equity and architecting your money flywheel.

Using the 3Bs Framework (Breaking In, Building Equity, and Breaking Out) to time your move to Building Equity allows you to step back and label where you are, where you want to go, and short-cut through years of detours and roadblocks on your way to MegaWealth.

Then, structuring your career into a money flywheel as soon as you enter the Building Equity phase supercharges your wealth-building opportunities, but few go down this path. They think it's scary when, in fact, it multiplies your opportunities by spreading out your bets.

Most people take the traditional route which they mistakenly view as "safe." Instead of architecting their money flywheels, which can seem scary, most people separate their career strategies from their investing strategies. They may hire career or life coaches, as I have in the past, or read mindset books, all to support their career ambitions. But, these coaches only move you forward on one plane.

The issue is that when you separate your career path from your investing strategy, you reduce your opportunity to experience step-function increases in your wealth.

What About Investing?

Industry icons like Warren Buffett and George Soros advise the average person to invest in the S&P index to earn 8% a year. But, that's not what made Buffett and Soros wealthy, and it's not what will make you wealthy. They made big bets (Buffett bet huge on Geico. Soros bet huge on the direction of the British Pound), and then they compounded off those wins.

Investing with your money flywheel activated is both a means to make more money (i.e., you expect returns from your angel and VC investments) and a networking strategy. As you network through your building and advising roles, you'll be offered opportunities to invest in exciting private companies. As you invest, you'll build stronger ties with talented founders, building up your network. Your career network and investing opportunity set will each drive the growth of the other one.

And yet, the common advice remains: advance in your career, step by step, while investing in the S&P index, keeping your career and investing separate. But that's not how big wealth is built.

Big wealth is being built in places like Silicon Valley, building, investing, and advising. People build equity early. They create personal money flywheels. It's second nature when everyone around you is doing the same thing.

The 3Bs Framework and money flywheel mentality makes this way of life second nature to you too, even if you weren't born in

Silicon Valley, even if you didn't grow up in the world of startups, VCs, and board directors.

The 3Bs Framework tells you where you are, guides you into building equity, and designs your money flywheel. Your money flywheel allows you to place multiple bets that could each pay off handsomely. With a bigger surface area of opportunities, you reduce your risk while increasing your upside potential. On Wall Street, we call that an asymmetric bet!

This is what the inner circles of Silicon Valley do, and there is nothing stopping you from doing the same... Except fear of the unknown. Fear of the unconventional path to building wealth.

Be bold. Break in. Build equity. Break out!

PART 2: HOW TO BUILD YOUR MONEY FLYWHEEL USING THE 3BS FRAMEWORK

CHAPTER 6: UNLOCKING THE BIG SILICON VALLEY SECRET

When I studied those who have made $100 million or more, witnessed several of my friends make $100 million by age 50, and worked closely with 5 billionaires (and known several more), the one thing I saw that separated success from failure was the

surface area of opportunity.

What do I mean by surface area of opportunity?

Surface area of opportunity is the sum of all the opportunities available to you. It's the best way to create your own luck. The larger the opportunity surface, the more chances you have to win.

Sam Altman, who has his own active money flywheel, expands on the idea of increasing your luck by increasing your surface area of opportunity:

"'Give yourself a lot of shots to get lucky' is even better advice than it appears on the surface. Luck isn't an independent variable but increases super-linearly with more surface area. You meet more people, make more connections between new ideas, learn patterns, etc." - Sam Altman, CEO OpenAI, former president of Y Combinator (YC).

◆◆◆

Building your money flywheel will allow you to experience the kind of luck that seems to happen regularly in Silicon Valley.

◆◆◆

With a money flywheel, you will increase your surface area of opportunity in three ways:

1. You operate in three realms, Build, Invest, Advise, so naturally you'll have more chances at step-function increases in wealth.

2. You meet more impressive people while working in Build, Invest, Advise rather than one job, which leads to more future opportunities.

3. Most importantly, *your money flywheel has network effects*. "Network Effect" generally means value increases as more people use it. For your money flywheel, networking with people who also have money flywheels means you cross-pollinate opportunities and luck. For instance, you'll benefit from the interactions of Build, Invest, Advise where investors may recommend you for a build role or an advisory role, your co-founder might introduce you to an investment opportunity, or your investor in one company may fund your next startup. The possibilities are nearly endless.

◆◆◆

As a funny aside, back in 1999, "network effects" was a popular descriptor for the business models of internet stocks that would skyrocket. I took this seriously and separated companies that I thought truly had them and those that didn't.

One day, I met Ross Perot as he was taking Perot Systems public through an IPO. I gave Ross my thesis on network effects. I told him it was originally called Metcalfe's Law because it was ideated by the founder of 3Com, Robert Metcalfe.

Ross said, "I know Bob! Would you like to speak with him?"

The next day, I gave Metcalfe my thesis on network effects as applied to internet stocks.

Metcalfe yelled through the phone, "THAT'S NOT WHAT I MEANT AT ALL!"

However, we still use the idea of network effects in both investing and business to express value increasing as components (members of the network) feed off each other.

Network effects between the components of your money flywheel is what makes your flywheel effective. An effective flywheel increases your chances of hitting $100 million in wealth.

Making $100 million is simple but not easy. It's simple math. Have an early exit of $5 million at age 23, compound it by 12% for 27 years, and you are worth $106 million by age 50.

But what if the average rate of return isn't 12%? What if you don't make $5 million by the early age of 23 and thus can't compound that $5 million for as long? That's where you need to have multiple exits along the way, each adding to the pie. Multiple exits are more likely when you increase the surface area over which you might experience these exits.

That's why, once you are in the Building Equity phase, it's critical to design, seed, and execute on your money flywheel so you can experience multiple exits in parallel. Exits from the companies you help build, the companies you invest in, and the companies you advise. You can work on all three, building, investing, and advising, at the same time.

Suddenly, you've increased your surface area of opportunity to succeed with your MegaWealth goals.

The 3Bs Framework (Breaking In, Building Equity, Breaking Out) gives you a map for where you are and where you want to go. As you move from Breaking In to Building Equity, you should purposefully build and seed your money flywheel, which increases both the probability of and number of future wealth events. Later, in Breaking Out, your money flywheel will be fully activated, generating multiple opportunities for liquidity events which can increase your wealth in a step-function manner.

Before Breaking Out, as soon as you enter the Building Equity phase and seed your money flywheel, you'll benefit from Human Network Effects - networking with interesting people in each segment of your flywheel to accelerate your progress in other segments of your flywheel.

Let's start with a more filled-out MegaWealth Flywheel to show you the types of roles you might pursue in each bucket of Build, Invest, and Advise. This one has typical jobs in each section of the flywheel. They are not your only options but are the ones I see the most often.

MegaWealth Money Flywheel with roles included

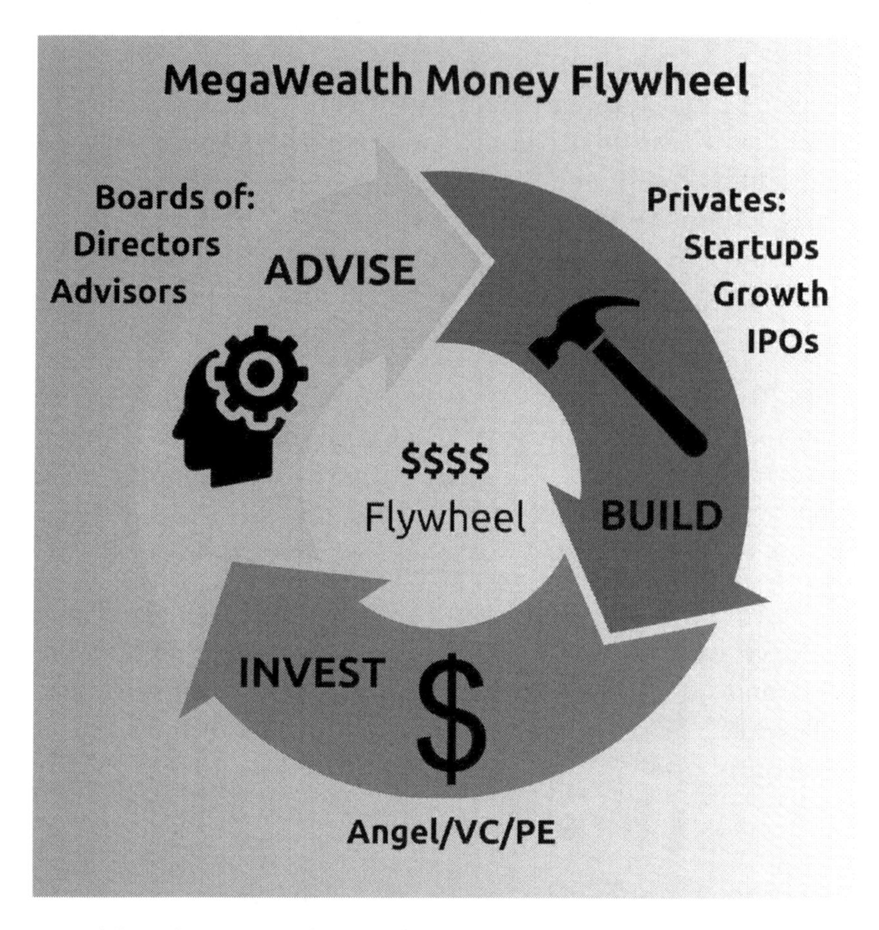

Just like the examples I shared in Chapter 4, your money flywheel will vary but will also have key components:

Build

You'll be building in return for equity plus salary. Typically, this means you are in a sales or leadership position where you can affect the growth of the company. This can be as a CEO, COO, or CMO and sometimes CFO of a higher profile company. You want to be front-facing, i.e., driving revenue growth. Revenue growth often has the biggest impact on company valuation. Your impact on growth and valuation will result in your being in high demand for your next Build position and, even more importantly, for the other two components of your money flywheel.

Invest

As part of the private market's ecosystem, you'll hear about interesting projects and have the opportunity to invest as an Angel investor (early-stage, individual investor who brings money, advice, and connections to the table). If selected carefully, those investments can have far higher returns than investing in public markets. Additionally, you'll be able to network with other highly connected angels. You may become a limited partner in several Venture Capital funds you get to know through your building activity. Depending on your overall goals, you'll join a later-stage VC or earlier-stage PE fund as a part-time partner, earning a percentage of the fund's returns while also networking for additional investments as well as your next Build role.

Advise

You'll join boards of advisors and, later, boards of directors of private companies. How do people get on boards? Companies will invite you to join these boards because you have already accomplished what they want to, but perhaps they can't afford you full time. Perhaps you grew sales from $10M to $50M at your last company. Then, a similar company wanting to expand from $10M to $50M might ask you to join their board as an independent director. Additionally, as a part-time partner at a VC or PE firm, they may ask you to join one or two boards of their portfolio companies. On these boards, you'll hear about additional leadership opportunities, investing opportunities, and board roles that you may be asked to consider.

We are all unique. Reflect on how different podcaster Tim Ferriss is from builder Elon Musk. You do not have to fit into a specific model when architecting your money flywheel, but you must build a flywheel that feeds on itself in a positive, compounding way.

As I explained in Chapter 4, Tim Ferriss' book and podcast is what he builds, and those projects help him network for additional investing and advising opportunities. Elon Musk focuses more on building than on advising, and the bulk of his investment returns come from him betting on himself by investing in the companies he builds.

My clients and friends are similar. They match what they're good at, either building, investing, or advising, lean into that component of their money flywheel more, and build differently based on their own strengths.

I will be here with you to help you figure out how to build your money flywheel in Part 3 of this book. The money flywheel is key to increasing your surface area of opportunity for MegaWealth, especially if you design it to maximize its network effects.

Next, here's how the money flywheel fits into the 3Bs Framework and your MegaWealth Plan:

Your MegaWealth Roadmap: from 3Bs, to Money Flywheel, to removing Roadblocks and building your MegaWealth Plan.

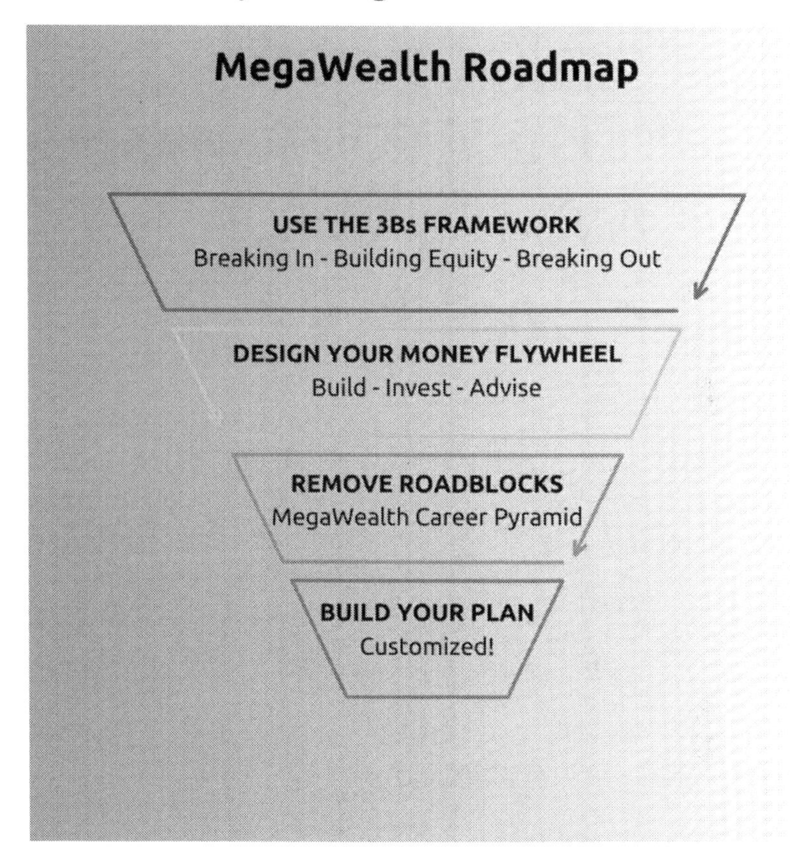

We will cover the step-by-step process of using the 3Bs Framework to build your MegaWealth Roadmap in Chapter 8. But first, before you can implement the 3Bs you're about to learn, you have to understand and overcome 3 hurdles. That way, you'll be set up to have the best chance at building MegaWealth.

CHAPTER 7: HOW TO PICK THE RIGHT INDUSTRY, COMPANY, AND TIMING FOR YOUR MEGAWEALTH PATH

Aside from mindset, which is covered in Chapter 9, the three biggest hurdles I see in trying to perfect your move from Breaking In to Building Equity and building your money flywheel are picking the right industry, joining the right company, and getting your timing right.

Let's look at those three hurdles.

Hurdle #1: Choosing the Right Industry

You may be like Bill Gurley in his early career: in a dead-end, non-vibrant industry, like PCs. How will you possibly figure out what industry to join and make your move, having to go through the Breaking In phase all over again before even thinking about your move to Building Equity? This all seems like it could be destabilizing for your family, career, and wealth.

As many of my clients say, once they see their map, they can't unsee it and nothing else makes sense. The 3Bs Framework will give you a mindset of evaluating industries and opportunities based on their inherent growth prospects, and before you know it, you'll be on a new trajectory.

How do you know if it's the "right" industry?

I've spent my career analyzing companies and industries. I like to combine proven methods of great investors, like Warren Buffett, George Soros, and Peter Lynch, along with great teachers, like Harvard's Michael Porter, with newer methods, like those of my billionaire bosses.

How to Spot a Promising Industry for Building Wealth.

An industry that can support your wealth generation should possess certain characteristics:

1. An industry should be large and growing faster than GDP (perhaps 5%-10% or more per year). Super fast growth (50%-100%+) will not be sustainable over more than a few years. That's the math.
2. An industry should score well on Michael Porter's 5 forces, which is very similar to what Warren Buffett calls a moat:
    a. It has good barriers to entry (not too competitive).
    b. It has low concentration (thus bargaining power) of buyers.
    c. It has easy barriers to exit (thus no irrational competitors who can't leave).
    d. It has low bargaining power of suppliers so your company won't get killed on costs.
    e. It has a low threat of new substitutes because what this industry creates is hard to replace with other items.

3. An industry should also possess the 3 elements my billionaire bosses looked for prior to investing: Catalyst, Timeliness, and Sustainability.

    a. There is a catalyst that created a positive change, increasing the industry's growth rate (higher demand or need, regulation, buying patterns).

    b. That positive change is timely, i.e., the change is occurring soon and investors are starting to recognize it. Never was the saying "If a tree fell and no one saw it, did it really happen?" more true than in investing.

    c. The positive change is sustainable over 5+ years. This is especially critical when you are choosing an industry to join for your career.

Self-Assessment: How bad is not starting in the right industry?

Rate yourself on a scale from 1 to 5 (1 = disagree, 5 = agree).

1. The industry I am in is not where I want to end up.
2. The industry I am in has little to no venture funding.
3. The industry I am in has little to no growth.

Now, add up your total score from all the questions above.

Surfing the Waves (3-6)

You are in an industry you find interesting with good growth and VC investment. Some of your scores might not be 1 out of 5, but you have enough good elements here to build your money flywheel (Chapters 6, 8, and 12). Remember, Bill Gurley was able to navigate into an ideal situation from an unattractive industry. My clients say that creating a plan using the 3Bs Framework reduces their anxiety.

Stuck in the Mud (7-15)

Being in a stagnant industry unrelated to where you want to go is tough. I know. I was there too. I started as a horse trainer and used my MBA to shift to investment management. It cost me time, but the biggest waste of time is not making a move. You may find Chapters 8 and 10 on moving from Breaking In to Building Equity, and Chapters 4, 6, 8, and 12 on building your money flywheel, inspiring for planning your future moves.

Hurdle #2: Choosing the Right Company

Your career is your single biggest investment.

How many people do you see join a new company for 10% more pay or because they are flattered by the offer? You know better. Your time is finite. You only have so many slots in your resume. Knowing this can add stress. How will you know if this is the ONE?

With the 3Bs Framework, you'll build a money flywheel. You'll have multiple income sources which can become multiple sources of large, financial exits. Your surface area of interesting opportunities will multiply so you don't need to count on one event to boost your wealth. Being in these high-achieving networks increases the likelihood you'll join a successful company.

When I think of the difference of choosing the right industry vs choosing the right company, I think of rivers, like those found in nature. The right industry is a healthy, fast-flowing river with lots of water. The right company is the best boat, able to travel down the river faster than other boats.

Fastest Boat on the Fastest, Healthiest River

The real magic happens when you get on the fastest, best boat in the fastest, healthiest river!

But, joining the best company as your first job rarely happens.

With my first couple of jobs, I would call my dad and tell him all the disastrous things that were happening, and he'd say, "Well, now you know how *not* to do it!" After a few of these chats, I finally blurted out, "I want to be somewhere where they are doing things right!" Nevertheless, we start where we start and then navigate to a better situation.

When trying to pick the best company to join, I assess both industries and companies along the same metrics: Porter's 5 forces, strong, healthy growth at the beginning of it's growth period (timely), positive change you can see and others are starting to recognize, a clear catalyst driving that positive change, and good reasons why this positive change is sustainable.

Remember, it's best to do this research ahead of time, not just in reaction to a job offer or recruiter inquiry. Know what industries and companies you would like to be part of. Build your skills and network to match what the industry and company needs.

When researching companies, don't forget the newer tools we have today, such as checking employer review sites like Glassdoor as well as doing searches on Google, Reddit, Twitter, and Crunchbase. You never know what you'll find!

Self-Assessment: How bad is picking the wrong company?

Rate yourself on a scale from 1 to 5 (1 = disagree, 5 = agree).

1. The company I am working at isn't doing well competitively.
2. The company I am working at keeps changing its strategy.
3. The company I am working at has trouble keeping people.

Now, add up your total score from all the questions above.

On a Rocket Ship (3-6)

Congrats! You are in a company with a solid strategy that is doing well and people like to work there. All of your scores might not be 1 out of 5, but you have enough good elements here to build your reputation, rack up some accomplishments, and supercharge your money flywheel (Chapters 4, 6, 8, and 12).

While it's great to pick the right company first, most successful entrepreneurs have 1-2 failed companies before they hit it big. Sam Altman, CEO of Open AI and former president of Y Combinator, had a first startup no one can remember. Same with Stuart Butterfield, founder of Slack. It only takes one big winner to change your outcome forever.

Down in the Dumps (7-15)

Being in the wrong company unrelated to where you want to go can be demoralizing. I remember the sinking feeling I felt when I walked through the door of my new employer only to find they had lied to me about the role I was offered, and worse, after 4 months, they told me I had to perform a role that involved breaking the law. I had no choice but to leave. Yet, that corporate experience and title led to my next higher-quality opportunity.

If you realize you're at the wrong company, it's best to balance creating too many short stints on your resume versus staying to rack up a few accomplishments you can point to. I do draw a hard line on breaking the law, and you should too. You may find Chapter 11 on researching to find the right industry and company useful as well as Chapters 7, 8, and 10 on timing your move from Breaking In to Building Equity. Chapters 4, 6, 8, and 12 on building your money flywheel can give you some inspiration for your future moves.

Whether or not your current company is "the one," using the money flywheel and 3Bs Framework will help you put where you are at into perspective.

Hurdle #3: Choosing the Right Timing

It may be nearly impossible to make the move to Building Equity at the right time for that industry, joining the right company at the right time for that company, and lining that up with what your ideal timing is in your career trajectory.

In fact, those who have hit the timing perfectly can become household names, like Bill Gates (Microsoft), Larry Ellison (Oracle), and Mark Zuckerberg (Facebook). If you started Microsoft or Oracle today, it would be too late and nearly impossible to succeed. There are theories that Gates and Ellison were born in the right years to found and lead the companies they did. How can you compete with that?

First, Gates and Ellison are outlier multibillionaires. There are approximately 720 billionaires in the US whereas there are 25,000 self-made households with over $100 million in wealth.

Understand the role of luck in timing.

I was lucky to start investing at 16 in 1982 right as we exited a deep recession. Stocks were cheap and poised to grow fast; a winning combination! I was also lucky to move into professional investing right out of my MBA at USC in 1994 and get the role of technology portfolio manager in 1996 and my own tech fund in 1998, riding the wave of internet fever. Had I started my career in investing 4 years later just before the 2000-2003 downturn, my fate could have been far different.

The right timing breaks down into several factors.

1. Economic Cycle Timing - Where are we in the growth of the economy? Are we in the early or late stages of

expansion? Are we entering a recession? Are we exiting a recession? Be careful not to constantly predict a recession and miss out on taking action and being a part of exciting industry growth. It's proven human nature to prioritize avoiding risk, and as such, we are drawn to pulling out early and forecasting doom.

2. Industry Timing - Is it early, but not too early, in the industry's growth? Early enough means there is plenty of growth ahead, not too much competition, and an opportunity for you to become influential in the industry. Too early means there isn't steady growth, investors come in and out without full commitment, and the future isn't clear.

3. Career Timing - Have you spent enough time in the Breaking In phase in order to show your contributions and be offered a role at a high-quality, private company? Does your own timing match up well with #1 and #2 above, or do you need a bit more time in Breaking In to attract higher-caliber, private company interest by building your accomplishments, network, and/or skill set?

With the 3Bs Framework, you'll have a model for what you are looking for along with the flexibility to speed up or slow down your own timing to align with your target industry and company. This isn't about perfection. Having the map will allow you to understand where you are and where you're going, which will put you ahead of most of your peers.

Self-Assessment: How bad is unideal timing of your move from Breaking In to Building Equity in your life really?

Rate yourself on a scale from 1 to 5 (1 = disagree, 5 = agree).

1. I worry that my move to Building Equity might result in me joining a low-quality company where my equity becomes worthless.
2. I am stuck in Breaking In and worry it is too late for me to move to Building Equity.
3. I am frozen, worried about making the move from Breaking In to Building Equity and am unsure if I am too early or too late.

Now, add up your total score from all the questions above.

Nothing but Green Lights (3-6)

You nailed your timing on one of the most difficult career moves. Kudos to you. Maybe it's not in an industry related to where you want to go, but you're moving in the right direction. Some of these might not be 1 out of 5, but you have enough elements here to build your money flywheel (Chapters 6, 7, and 11). Remember, Meg Whitman lost decades in her timing and still became a billionaire. Using the proven 3Bs Framework is the first step to mastering your timing.

Deer in Headlights (7-15)

Making a move from Breaking In to Building Equity is a bit like Goldilocks and the Three Bears. You could be too early and end up at a low-quality company, too late and lose a year or more of progress, or maybe right on time but unsure in your decision... All these are stressful situations. If you are at a lower-quality company, make a positive difference and use that accomplishment to move to a higher-quality one.

Yes, Peter Thiel regrets staying in the Breaking In phase too long and not becoming an entrepreneur earlier, but he's still a successful billionaire entrepreneur. I also regret delaying my move to Building Equity by 14 years, but I still made the move and love the life I have built as a result. You may not get your timing perfect, but the fact that you are thinking about it puts you ahead of 99% of your peers.

If you moved too late like me, make the best of it. Moving forward with positive action starting today will feel great. You may find Chapter 10 on timing and Chapters 7, 8, and 14 on moving from Breaking In to Building Equity inspirational.

Moving from Breaking In to Building Equity and then structuring your ideal money flywheel is doable. It's not easy, but definitely doable. The 3Bs Framework shows you where you are and reminds you to keep moving forward, the money flywheel shows you where you are going, and the Wealth Pyramid helps you remove any obstacles in your way.

Part 2 describes how this process can work for you.

CHAPTER 8: HOW TO BUILD MEGAWEALTH, STEP BY STEP

Step #1 - Use the 3Bs Framework to Navigate Your Career.

The 3Bs Framework is both powerful and easy to understand. Execution is key, but with this framework, you'll know where you are and where you need to go. You'll also be able to learn from other people's successful careers using this framework.

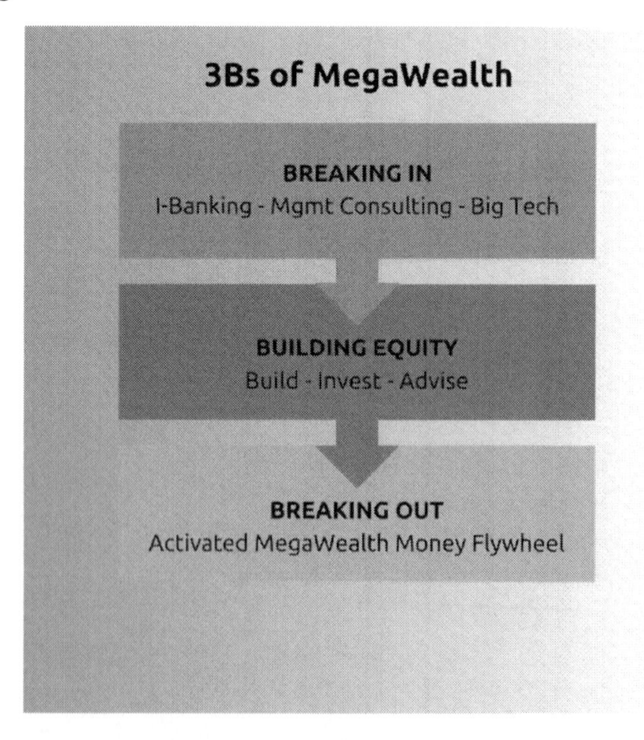

1. Breaking In

Breaking into any career is hard. The focus of this book is how to break into careers that could, along with your investing, result in $100 million in wealth or more. Investment banking, management consulting, and working at a large tech company (Google, Apple, Amazon, Facebook, etc.) are great foundational careers to break into because they can feed into startup equity, venture capital, private equity, and board of director roles.

Whether or not you were that 16-year-old with perfect grades who made it to the Ivy Leagues and bulge bracket investment banks, it's probably not too late to break in.

First, there are many paths to wealth. Second, there are more private companies than public ones. The private market space is enormous, and it is filled with opportunities, including private equity investment banks, like Lincoln International, plenty of startups at various stages, and consulting firms that will hire you later in life for your expertise.

The most direct path to breaking in is through investment banking and management consulting straight out of college. If this isn't possible for you, consider your personality and unique skills. How might you gain similar experiences through creative paths?

I missed nearly all the onramps. I went to a state school instead of an Ivy or Stanford. I rode horses in the Junior Olympics rather than getting summer internships. After college, I became a full-time horse trainer. I later transitioned my career by getting my MBA at age 26. Five years later, I was running the #1 fund in the world.

As I mentioned before, my second big miss was after running that #1 fund and working for the top hedge fund at the time, I failed to leverage those high profile accomplishments to make the transition to Building Equity. I delayed that move by 14 years!

My misses are why I am writing this book: so you stay as long as necessary but as short as possible in the Breaking In phase. Stand in your value, move to Building Equity, and activate your money flywheel!

2. Building Equity

Moving from Breaking In to Building Equity is one of the hardest, scariest, and potentially most rewarding moves you can make to build your wealth. You are taking a risk by accepting part equity and part salary for your time. You could likely earn a far higher salary at a bigger company. However, if you choose the private company well, your equity could be worth more than you'd earn working the rest of your life at that larger company.

Building equity typically happens when you join a fast-growing, VC-funded private company. You can also build equity when you take equity as part of your compensation as a board director or advisor. And, if your chosen primary path is as an investor, taking part of the fund profits ("carry") will help you build wealth not by the hours you work but as a function of how much clients invest with you. That's what we professional investors call "OPM" or Other People's Money.

In the Building Equity phase (Congrats. If you are already building equity, then this section can show you how to maximize the returns on your efforts.), your wealth has the opportunity to move up in a step-function manner independent from how much you invest your time or money.

How do you get your wealth to increase in big steps rather than slowly over time? Simple, but not easy...

When I finally decided to make the move to Building Equity, I was told that I was "too senior for my lack of experience." I was 51 with no corporate experience. But still, that hurt, so I doubled down, taking a 6-month coding bootcamp at UC Berkeley to modernize my resume.

Then, I caught a break. A business associate (he was a former CFO of a company I had invested in as part of my portfolio management career) reached out and offered me a job. I've stayed active on LinkedIn and I write a MegaWealth newsletter, so I was front of mind for him. He offered me a VP role at a cryptocurrency ATM network where he was COO and CFO. It was a management stepping stone with zero equity.

Next, I had been networking with some smart people in startups. I had invested in one. The CEO of that startup asked me to be an expert on a panel discussion on privacy in 2020. One of the other panel members was a serial entrepreneur. After my VP role in 2021, the other panel member and I started talking, and he hired me as his COO for his startup. Now, I have had 3 COO roles in startups, advise and invest in other startups, and have my money flywheel activated.

I do NOT recommend my path. It does show you that you can make it even if you have missed multiple onramps! Yes, it's harder to get to $100 million, or your version of MegaWealth, the later you start. But, there is always a path to separating your time spent from money earned, and I will help you find yours.

How do you know when you are ready to make the move from Breaking In to Building Equity?

Make your move as soon as possible, but wait as long as necessary.

First, start Building Equity as soon as possible because you'll have more time to compound your returns, get more chances at wealth, and have more fun in this dynamic private company world.

Second, wait as long as necessary to get the right opportunity. Some, like Marc Andreessen, were building in college and immediately started a company. Peter Theil likely feels he built his foundation and stayed in the Breaking In phase for too long. (Thus, now he pays students to drop out of college if they have an idea worth building.) Bill Gurley needed time to reposition himself by moving into his preferred area of internet platform banking before making the move into Building Equity as a venture capital partner.

How will you know when the timing is right for you? My clients find that they may have to give up a bit of pay for more equity, but they are being recruited by top quality firms. Most importantly, they are not working for only equity.

If only lower-quality startups are willing to hire you or companies want you to work for only equity, these are signs that you may need to build up a better track record and LinkedIn presence for a bit longer before moving into the Building Equity phase. Stand in your value.

The risk in moving too early is you may string together a bunch of 9-18 month stints at lower-quality companies, which won't attract VC or PE interest in your skills, nor will it allow you to be considered for high quality boards. This will make it nearly impossible to build your money flywheel.

So, stay as long as necessary and as short as possible in Breaking In before moving to Building Equity. In Chapter 7 on industries and Chapter 10 on timing, you can dive deeper into how to execute this most critical move. You won't lose your notes in the margins of this book, never to be found again. You'll use these foundational elements as part of your MegaWealth Plan, putting it together as you go through the material, using the downloadable PDF MegaWealth Workbook (Chapter 15).

Moving into Building Equity doesn't mean joining a tiny, 3-person startup like I did. There are many models to fit your personality. Frank Slootman, CEO of Snowflake and former CEO of ServiceNow, made billions by preparing private companies for their IPOs and leading them as their post-IPO CEO in the public markets.

3. Breaking Out

Breaking Out is where the huge money is made, but it doesn't necessarily mean starting your own company. It refers to betting on yourself.

In the Breaking Out phase, all your equity building seeds are starting to bear fruit. Your money flywheel is whirring along. You have roles as a builder, investor, and advisor, and you have levers to move your time where it drives the highest returns.

Hundreds of millions are made by increasing the surface area of opportunities via the MegaWealth Money Flywheel.

When you look at huge money made, in the hundreds of *billions*, successful founders win the biggest prizes. Obvious examples include Bill Gates starting Microsoft or Elon Musk with Tesla or SpaceX.

However, 90% of startups fail within 5 years. For every Bill Gates and Elon Musk, there is a wide graveyard of founders and startup executives who were underpaid for years hoping to make it back in equity which fell to zero.

What if you don't want to start your own company from scratch or even at all? There are still plenty of paths to MegaWealth available to you. Bill Gurley joined Benchmark and built his money flywheel around investing and advising. He didn't start his own company, yet today he is worth over $7 billion.

Now that I've explained how the 3Bs Framework helps you figure out where you are, how will you use it? Step 1 (3Bs) Takeaways are designed to reflect how you can use the 3Bs in your life.

Step 1 (3Bs) Takeaways:

1. Figure out where you are and where you want to be in the 3Bs.

2. Start thinking about how and when to make your moves.

3. Even if your timing, industry selection, and company selection aren't perfect, this can be offset by increasing your surface area of opportunity through your money flywheel.

The key to moving from Breaking In to Building Equity to Breaking Out is seeding your MegaWealth Money Flywheel as you enter the Building Equity phase and fully activating it in the Breaking Out phase.

Let's take a look at how you to design your money flywheel in the context of the 3Bs Framework in Step #2.

Step #2 - Build Your Money Flywheel

You should purposefully build the foundations of your money flywheel as soon as you enter the Building Equity phase of the 3Bs Framework. You've seen this money flywheel before... I'm including it here so it's easy to find.

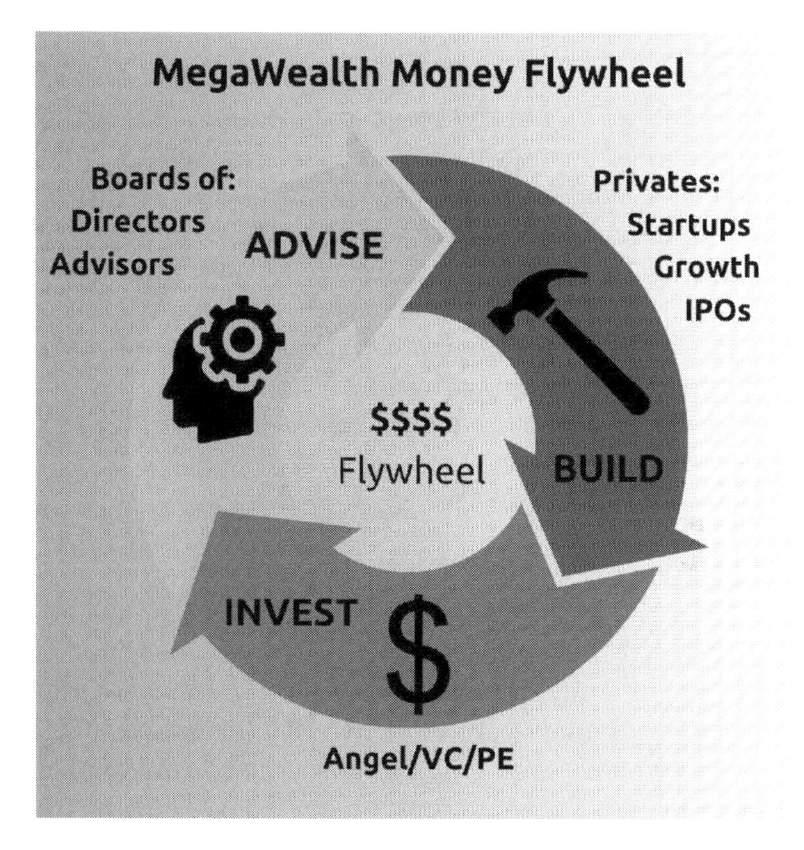

If this is the typical money flywheel, how will your money flywheel look?

Build

Typically, but not always, your money flywheel starts when you get a role in the Build portion. Grab leadership roles where you can show P&L responsibility and the ability to prove you grew a company from, say, $50M to $150M, or start by growing a company from $10M to $50M. How do you grow a company? By being head of sales, CMO, CEO, or even COO or CFO, but those last two are less regarded as customer-facing and are viewed as not having as much impact on revenue growth. Remember, you are building a track record of success. Each success can build on the last one, step by step.

Invest

Network with the VCs of the company where you are growing their portfolio company's topline or P&L. Investors will value the connection and conversation. You may become a trusted advisor, scout or part-time partner for a VC or PE fund. Those who were investors in some of the companies you grew can become future partners and sources of new opportunities. At this PE or VC fund, as a part-time partner, you can be paid "carry," which is a percentage of the profits of the fund, thereby building another source of equity in parallel to your "day job" of growing a private company.

Advise

Boards of other companies looking to grow from $50M to $150M or from $10M to $50M will want you on their boards of directors to guide them through the same process. VC and PE funds who get to know you may invite you on boards of their portfolio companies, especially if you are a part-time partner of their fund. Many VCs are on multitudes of boards as it is their fiduciary duty to their own investors, but they are stretched thin and this gives you an opportunity to gain board roles and experience.

Above, I have mapped out a traditional money flywheel.

There Are Three Ways Your Money Flywheel May Differ.

1. Overemphasize your strengths by placing more time in one of the three areas (Build, Invest, Advise).

The Investor

Bill Gurley has one job as a VC at Benchmark. He invests the bulk of his wealth through his fund. His board roles are part of his job at his fund. He spends his time in the Invest part of the flywheel, not in the Build section. (I.e., he is not personally building startups but does advise and invest in startups that are being built.)

The Builder

My friend, Jenny, was a great biotech builder. She took her first company public as a Chief Medical Officer and the second one as a CEO. She is in high demand as a board member to guide other biotechs along the same paths. Now, she invests money earned from both her board and build roles. She has exceeded $100 million by focusing her efforts on building.

The Advisor

Another friend of mine, Shelby, started in investment banking and made a lucrative first career there. Rather than move into building like I did, she was offered and took a Board of Director position. One role led to the next, and her money flywheel revolves around advising and investing with zero building.

When you think through your personality (values, traits, and purpose) in the MegaWealth Pyramid, you may find you gravitate towards one part of the flywheel over the other. That's the point. Make it your own. Just be sure to move to that area because it's your strength rather than avoid another part of the flywheel because it's something you fear.

2. Change what it means to invest or build (podcasts, angels, etc.)

When I showed you the typical MegaWealth Money Flywheel, I mentioned that, although this is typical, it is not the rule.

The advising portion of the flywheel has fewer variations than the investing or building portions. On the advising portion of the flywheel, you can either be on a board of directors or a board of advisors. When comparing the two, the board of directors is harder to join, pays more, and has more liability.

In the investing portion and building portion, there are many variations.

As an investor, some start as an angel and stay that way (Tim Ferriss), and others migrate over time to scouting for a VC, being a subject matter expert for a PE fund, or even being a part-time venture partner or PE partner. In deciding what you'll do, match your skills and personality to what those funds might want. If you are a long-term growth person, think late-stage VC, especially if that is the stage of company you want to lead as a builder. If you are a deal person where you tend to think about the entire ecosystem of competitors, the entire cap table of each company, and you have a background in investment banking, then private equity may be a better focus for you.

As a builder, you may be a serial entrepreneur, but many are not. Many executives and board members focus on preparing private companies for their IPO debut. Owning equity in this transition can be very lucrative, and building doesn't necessarily mean a company. What it does mean is *leverage*. Build where you have a one-to-many relationship, which will allow any equity you earn to increase in value faster. This one-to-many relationship can be expressed in software (build once, sell infinitely), entertainment (movies, actors, producers, podcasts, books), and finance (banking, investment management).

As you can see, there are enough choices for everyone in the build portion of your money flywheel. Make sure your role has leverage in that it separates your time from wealth, and be sure what you are building has natural leverage.

3. Align the timing of your target industry's growth with the entry of the type of investor you want to join.

Designing your money flywheel in a vacuum separate from reality won't work. If your invest section includes angel investing, that will need to align with an emerging, earlier-stage industry you want to join on the build side to best leverage your network and information across the sections of your money flywheel.

If you want to join a more stable growing private company that is VC funded, then you may do some angel investing but should also consider becoming an LP (limited partner) in several VC funds for financial and networking returns.

If you decide you are more of a deal person and want to align with private equity, even though they are often side by side on cap tables with late-stage VC funds, this will require a different strategy. You'll need to enter the target industry (where the PE firm is investing) early enough to be thought of as one of the leaders, yet not so early that you have to wait too long for the industry to become large enough for private equity to invest.

The power in your MegaWealth Money Flywheel is unleashed when the 3 sections (Build, Invest, Advise) amplify the positive impacts of each other. You can make it your own, even going as far as being a podcaster for your build section. Just make sure you create it with this amplification designed in.

Step #2 (Money Flywheel) Takeaways:

1. The common factor in profitable money flywheels is the interaction between the 3 areas of Build, Invest, and Advise. Make sure yours are complementary and positively amplifying each other.

2. The best money flywheels combine being in good industries, selecting good companies, and having attractive investment opportunities. For more on selecting good industries and companies, see Chapter 7.

3. While there are common traits of the best money flywheels, the only money flywheel that will work for you is one that fits with your strengths, personality, and purpose.

To make sure your flywheel is able to work for you at full force, you need to use your MegaWealth Pyramid to remove any roadblocks to success.

Step #3: Remove any Roadblocks to Success Using Your MegaWealth Pyramid

The MegaWealth Pyramid helps you build your strongest foundation. This foundation lets you go as far as you desire, and perhaps even farther than you dared to dream. It also helps remove any roadblocks to your success. So, what's the catch?

Focusing on the foundational layer, health, is the step where I get the most pushback from my coaching clients. When I ask about their sleep or exercise or connections at home, they argue that it's not about their careers or wealth - which is what they want coaching on. However, after the initial resistance, they complete this step and find it to be most fundamental, necessary, and valuable to their long-term success.

Here's a look at the MegaWealth Pyramid

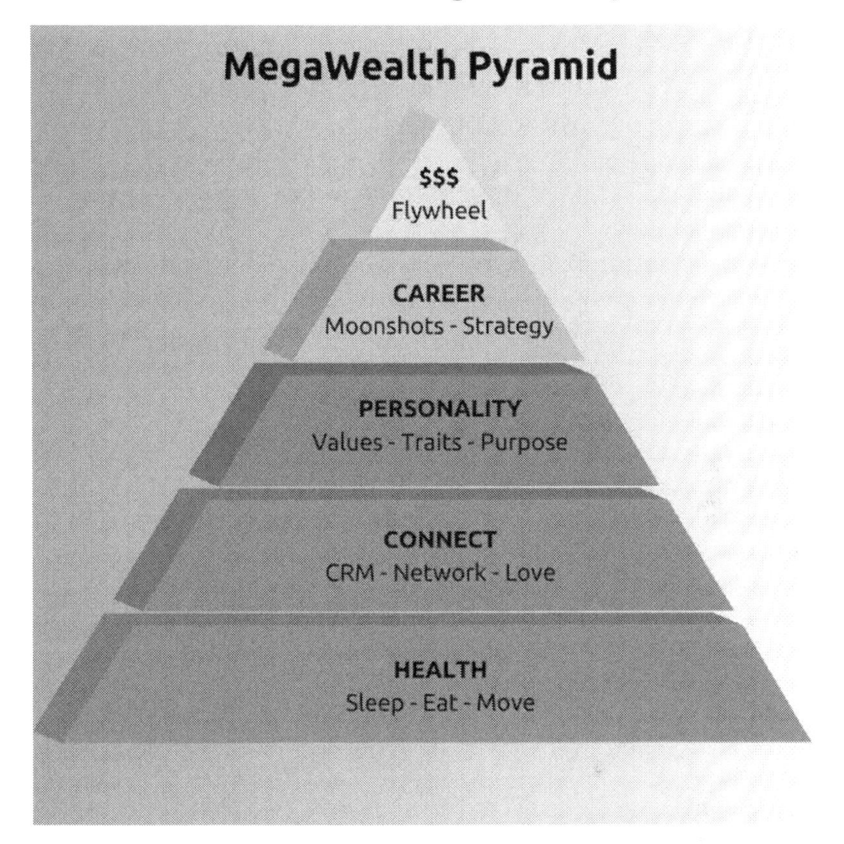

Like any pyramid, it is only as strong as its foundation. The best way to use this MegaWealth Pyramid is to start at the bottom. Only move up to the next layer when the layers below it are functioning well. If something on a higher layer starts to falter, for instance your career, look to the lower layers for holes you can fix (networking, connection, health, values, etc.).

Now, I will describe each layer. In Chapter 13, I will take you through your own pyramid using the downloadable PDF MegaWealth Workbook. For now, I'm describing what the Pyramid is so you can see how it fits into the process of building MegaWealth.

Foundational Layer 1: Health

Embarking on a multiyear or multidecade Wealth Plan involving big goals and hard work requires stamina and good judgment. These come from a foundation of good sleep, nutrition, and exercise. Furthermore, if you skip over your health, you may build wealth but not be able to enjoy it due to poor health.

Sleep is foundational. I've found that I make better nutrition and exercise choices when I get enough rest. For me, sleep comes first. Second, if I eat well, then I have more energy and positivity to exercise. That is how I rank my health areas, and most of my clients feel the same.

For sleep, I find the following helps: regular bedtime, no sugar after noon, no food 3 hours before bedtime, and sleep on a firm mattress in a dark, quiet, cool room. For nutrition, I focus on getting enough protein, eating whole foods, and avoiding sugar, junk food, and processed foods. I also take supplements which are customized for my needs. For exercise, try and move at least 30 minutes per day doing something you enjoy. Do something that's easy to take on the road so you minimize excuses.

Foundational Layer 2: Connect

Networking can be overwhelming and scary, but it is the only way to get where you want to go. You can't go it alone. Additionally, a major part of your mental and physical health is tied to feeling positive connections, both personal and professional.

The biggest stresses I hear from clients at the connect layer are: I don't know how to network, I have the wrong network, and I am worried I will lose touch with my spouse as I build my career. Not to worry. I've got you covered!

Worries about how to connect and build networks are so widespread that I dedicated Chapter 9: The Connected Mind to this topic. I describe how to connect most effectively, both professionally and personally.

Foundational Layer 3: Personality

In order to have the most staying power to pursue your goals (and possibly have some fun along the way), you need to figure out how your personality will best align with your ideal career and wealth path. Take time to clarify your values, compare your values with the personality traits necessary for people going after your same goals, and align these with your sense of purpose. This foundational step is one my clients often want to skip but the one that yields them (and will yield you) the greatest benefits.

In this step, spend time thinking about what values you live by today and which ones you want to take forward with you. Next, look at the traits you need to be successful when your money flywheel is operational. You'll decide if you need to improve on any traits, and more importantly, if your values and desired traits are aligned. Finally, you'll define your purpose, which will be your mental and spiritual engine to keep you pushing forward towards your goals.

Clarity on your values, traits, and purpose will help you choose focus areas when building your own money flywheel.

Layer 4: Career

A big roadblock I see preventing people from generating maximum wealth from their career is they don't dream big enough.

JFK gave his famous "We choose to go to the Moon." speech at Rice University on the nation's space effort in 1962 to bolster public support for his proposal to land a man on the Moon and bring him safely back to Earth before 1970. In 1962, we were lacking many of the technologies that were needed to accomplish this goal. JFK's moonshot goal catalyzed one of the most innovative periods of technological advancement ever.

People tend to overestimate their capabilities in the short run, but they far underestimate their potential in the long-term. Why? We are famously bad at understanding the power of compounding. Our brains think in a more linear fashion, but our efforts at networking, building, and investing all compound.

Underestimating your potential is like a death knell. If you don't build big enough goals, you'll hit your goals and lose motivation. I've seen this play out many times. It takes tremendous effort to reinvigorate yourself towards new, bigger goals. You can lose years of momentum.

I met Anky van Grunsven two weeks after she won her second individual Olympic Gold medal in Dressage (equestrian) for the Netherlands. The Germans had won the Dressage Olympic team gold every year for 50 years straight, so it was unheard of to win one gold, much less two Olympics in a row. Was she elated? No. She was depressed. She had so overshot her goals she didn't have anything else to work towards. Eventually, she remotivated herself and won yet another Olympic Gold on a new horse, but the effort and depression she experienced in between were avoidable.

I also didn't dream big enough in my career. Now, I help people avoid making the same mistake. Moonshot your goals, and have doable milestones to celebrate along the way.

Layer 5: $$$ Flywheel

Your money flywheel is at the top of your MegaWealth Pyramid. If you have holes that need fixing in your foundation, executing on your money flywheel will be much harder or even impossible. If your flywheel isn't working, go back to your lower layers to figure out what's holding you back.

When your foundational layers are functioning well, you are healthy, energetic, connected, and your actions are aligned with your traits, values, and purpose, then you know where you are headed. Building your flywheel becomes a natural extension of who you are and what you do.

This chapter has a separate section on building your flywheel. Remember, it is easier to build and run your money flywheel when you don't have any big roadblocks or fatal holes in your MegaWealth Pyramid. In Chapter 13, you'll go through a series of assessments to make sure your MegaWealth Pyramid is roadblock free!

Step #3 (Wealth Pyramid) Takeaways:

1. Always start at the bottom of the pyramid. A pyramid is only as strong as its foundation. If there are problems with your sleep or health, fix those first. If things start to falter in your life or career plan, go back to the bottom layer and fix issues there, then move up layer by layer.

2. This is not about being perfect or fixing everything. This pyramid is finding the things you think are holding you back, i.e., where you rate yourself as sub-par and want to improve that area. Don't let this pyramid be an excuse for naval gazing, perfectionism, or procrastination.

3. Know you don't have to fix everything at once. You can set priorities and include steps for improvement in your overall career plan.

Now that you know where you are in the 3Bs, have designed your money flywheel, and have made a plan to remove any obstacles to your goals, it's time to learn how to map out your MegaWealth Plan.

Step #4 - Map Your Career and Wealth Plan

As a reminder, you'll build your own MegaWealth Plan using the downloadable PDF workbook. This chapter describes the process.

Finally, with most of the hard work done, you'll build your MegaWealth map. You know what your moonshot goal is using your 3Bs Framework, you understand how your money flywheel will look, and you have a list of roadblocks to remove.

Now, you'll put your goals, money flywheel, and roadblocks to remove into a plan.

You'll build a quarterly, annual, and 5-year plan of execution and milestones towards your moonshot goal using the 3Bs Framework and money flywheel as guides.

Your plan will include your moonshot goals with a date to reach those goals. Then, in each of the next quarters and years, you'll fill in plans to improve holes in your MegaWealth Pyramid.

Next, insert your career milestones on the way to your big goals.

You'll include rough career milestones that move you into Building Equity, or if you are already there, then career milestones that execute on your MegaWealth Money Flywheel. What is the timing and strategy of your move to Building Equity? What industry and target companies do you have in mind? When do you think you will make each move?

Finally, track your progress.

You'll track how you are doing via plan, revisit your MegaWealth Pyramid to see if any new roadblocks need addressing, analyze how your MegaWealth Money Flywheel is serving you, and keep moving along the 3Bs Framework. You won't predict this perfectly and will keep adjusting, but it's far better to have a map and a destination in mind.

Step #4 (MegaWealth Plan) Takeaways:

1. While making the plan may seem mundane when compared to the first 3 steps, this is where the rubber meets the road.

2. The magic happens when you combine massive moonshot goals with achievable milestones to celebrate. Take the time to complete this plan using the downloadable PDF MegaWealth Plan Workbook.

3. Plans are useless if not reviewed against actual events and revised regularly. Treat yours as a living document.

Congratulations for making it through the 3Bs! Now you have everything you need to get to where you want to be wherever you might be on your journey to $100 million wealth.

I know you just consumed a lot of information, so if you feel overwhelmed, excited, confused, or all of the above, it's totally normal. My team and I are here to answer any questions you might have and chat about where you are on your journey. Just schedule a call: https://calendly.com/emmy-sobieski/15-minute-intro-call

CHAPTER 9: HOW TO HAVE A MEGAWEALTH MINDSET

In addition to what I have shared previously in this book (navigating the 3Bs Framework, building your Wealth Pyramid, and structuring your money flywheel), there are 3 Critical Components you must master to maximize your chances for success.

1. Your mindset
2. Your timing
3. Your investing

In the next 3 chapters, I will show you how to master all three with respect to your MegaWealth goal.

I have worked closely with 5 billionaires for years. I am grateful to have spent so much time learning from them. Their mindsets are optimized for building wealth.

Wikipedia defines mindset as: "An established set of attitudes of a person or group concerning culture, values, philosophy, frame of mind, outlook, and disposition. It may also arise from a person's worldview or beliefs about the meaning of life."

Within this definition of mindset, what will help accelerate you towards your MegaWealth goal?

Here are shared mindsets of the billionaires and ultra-wealthy that have helped them on their paths to wealth. For optimal results, you need to master all 4 mindsets with the beginner mind being the most critical.

1. Beginner Mind

All 5 billionaires I worked for had well-honed beginner minds. They asked the most basic questions and were unattached to the answers. This saves time and energy that comes from making assumptions. My hedge fund boss, Glenn, would walk into a room with a management team and simply ask, "How's it going?" and they'd tell him! Mike Milken, who made over a billion dollars in four years as an investment banker in the late 1980s, also had a well-tuned beginner mind and asked short, simple questions.

A beginner mind is not a growth mindset.

Scarcity and negative mindsets also work fine. They help avoid losses and risks by researching longer and saying no more often.

Even those wealthy-negative, scarcity-mindset people I know well have beginner minds. Someone with a beginner mind is willing to start from zero, assume they don't know anything, and ask very basic questions.

A beginner mind has multiple benefits in building MegaWealth.

You don't assume anything. Many great startups were born by asking if something we always did a certain way could be done differently. Same goes for improving efficiency, changing strategy, and listening to customers. There is an incredible, unlimited power in the ability to ask the beginner "dumb" question.

For the purposes of building MegaWealth, strengthen your beginner mindset. Practice asking shorter, open-ended questions. Let the other person talk more. Ask questions you don't know the answer to. Question yourself on what you really know. At each turn, try to peel back the onion, asking more and more fundamental questions.

Ask customers, bosses, employees, family, and friends. Practice your beginner mindset early and often. Build that mental muscle. You'll be amazed by what you learn and the opportunities that appear.

Remember, the purpose of a question is not to make yourself sound smart (long, complicated questions) but to both connect and learn. For this, use five-to-seven-word, open-ended, non-leading questions and watch your world expand!

2. Neutral Mind

Although it isn't the case that each mindset builds on the one before, it is easier to have a neutral mind once you have mastered the beginner mindset. The late Trevor Moawad worked with top athletes, including the NFL quarterback Russell Wilson. He focused on removing negative thoughts through neutral thinking rather than positive thinking.

The billionaires I worked with used their beginner mindsets to hone their neutral minds. For instance, Milken used to ask me to look into various companies. He never told me ahead of time what he was thinking. He was waiting for the evidence to come in and wanted to remain impartial until he could weigh the pros and cons. The opposite is someone thinking they love a certain stock and only truly hear additional news or analysis about that stock if it is positive.

Neutral thinking is a middle ground, impartial and unbiased. Instead of encouraging purely positive thoughts, neutral thinking is a judgment-free, high-performance strategy that places emphasis on how you respond to evidence as it arrives along with how you control your thoughts.

Moving forward, be mindful of the thoughts you let get embedded in your mind, question them with a neutral stance, and get rid of any that don't serve you (by entertaining their opposites as possibilities) before they become feelings and, later, actions that don't serve you.

Learning how to act with a neutral mind and knowing when to quit will allow you to compound your wins while minimizing your losses on the way to MegaWealth.

To build a neutral mind, observe your thoughts and feelings as well as how you listen to others. Take in information like a scientist. Just the facts. Don't attach emotion. Decide based on pros and cons.

This takes practice but will make you a better decision maker.

3. Present Mind

Once you have a grounded beginner and neutral mind, the next step is to live in the present. This may sound counterintuitive because this entire book is about building a plan for your future, but if you live in the past or in the future, you'll be less effective in this moment.

All 5 billionaires I worked for rarely looked back with regret or forward with worry. When I came into work, they had plenty that needed to be analyzed and acted on the here and now. They were moving forward every day while their competitors were stressing about the past and future, thus falling behind.

This moment is the only one you can act in. It's the only one where you can make changes and push yourself, and your wealth, forward.

The trick is to build your map just like you have done in building your career path using the 3Bs so you know where you are going. Then, let that go in order to focus 100% on what you need to get done today to increase your speed and the probability of achieving your long-term goals.

Although an oversimplification, it is often said that those who dwell on the past are prone to depression and regret and those who focus on the future are prone to worry and anxiety. What is true is that you can't change the past or the future, and knowing that can be stressful. You can act now to change your direction which can change where you end up.

With MegaWealth, you build a future map but live in the present day to work towards the goals on your map. It is easier said than done, but try to be attached to doing your best and caring about your output but detached from the outcome (which you can't 100% control).

Each day, ask yourself, "What is the one thing I can do today to move me forward towards my goals the most?" Do that first.

Having a plan allows you to maximize the positive impact of the present moment because your actions are driving you in a direction you have chosen. Don't let this draw you into thinking only about the future. Stay focused on what you can do today, and rest assured that having a plan will allow you to spot the moments for change. Rely on your habit of daily action to get you where you want to go.

4. Connected Mind

You can't get to big wealth alone. The billionaires I worked with and my friends who made $100 million by age 50 all focused on networking on a daily basis. They had it in a system. It was second nature to reach out to people, include people, and get their opinions. They are also ultra focused on who they spend time with. Their circle of the 5 people they spend the most time with are carefully curated, brilliant, and influential people.

Feeling connected is key to your MegaWealth Pyramid.

Connection drives health and happiness with friends and family. Your ability to network, effectively connecting with others, is the engine that will drive your success. But often, when I advise my clients to build out their network, they worry. They think they aren't good networkers or don't know how to do it without sounding transactional or pushy.

I asked one of my best friends her secret to being an incredible networker and salesperson. "I just love people," she said. Simple yet powerful.

From that day, I started each interaction by trying to trust and love people. I purposefully told myself I was looking forward to meeting them and learning what was unique about them. The more I created this new reality in my mind, the more interesting people became.

The real secret to being a great networker is to leverage micro-moments of connection. This means you focus 100% of your attention on the other person for a moment, maybe 30 seconds to a few minutes. This strategy has been shown to build connection between people far faster than hours together of partly paying attention to the other person. Using this strategy will benefit both your professional network and your relationships with friends and family.

With that foundation of curiosity and love for people, change how you network and interact with others one micro-moment at a time.

Here's a quick example of how to do it. Give a person at a meeting, a party, or on the phone 100% of your undivided attention. Really listen. Mirror what they say by telling them what you heard. Ask 1-2 follow-up questions to learn more.

People become more interesting when you are interested. What's the big secret here? You seem more interested when you are a skilled, active listener.

When you study people who have built great wealth, from Elon Musk, to Mark Zuckerberg, to Steve Jobs, you'll learn that they were part of a community of other like-minded entrepreneurs.

Build your community of your 5 closest friends with purpose, using micro-moments of connection.

Warning: Mindset work can be a powerful accelerator or a crutch.

Mindset is a very popular topic in general, especially with respect to building wealth. Why? Yes, it can be effective, but people can use mindset work as a way to procrastinate real work while still feeling a sense of accomplishment.

You only have so many hours in the day. While a certain amount of time should be spent on health, values, and reflecting, too much time spent working "on" yourself and your career versus working "in" your career can be detrimental. Once you have a strategy, the biggest thing you can do is take action, moving forward every day, not continually researching mindsets, strategies, and other ideas.

Procrastinating using mindset work as an excuse is popular. When looking at books on how to create wealth and investing books, the #1 method is to have a money mindset. As an institutional investor with 25 years of experience managing billions of dollars in assets, I can tell you firsthand that having a money mindset is not enough.

Yes, you need the right mindset, but remember, it is only one component of the bigger picture. Mindset alone will not get you to MegaWealth. Following the 3Bs Framework, auditing your Wealth Pyramid, and building your money flywheel are all necessary components, along with mastering your mindset, timing, and investing.

The Four $100 Millionaire Mindsets Key Takeaways:

1. Start with the beginner mind, asking open-ended questions.
2. Build a neutral mind, being open to data like a scientist.
3. Use a present mind to get more done, regret less, and worry less.
4. With a connected mind, your network becomes your net worth!

The next critical component after your mindset is mastering your timing.

CHAPTER 10: HOW TO HAVE MEGAWEALTH TIMING

Great timing is often mistaken for luck. What person is going to explain that it wasn't luck but rather an ability to perfectly time their move? They'd seem arrogant.

We assume it's luck, and they let us.

MegaWealth Timing is the optimal use of time. It's not about maximizing your efficiency so you can fill your calendar to the max. Optimal use of time includes periods of deep work, periods of rest and reflection, and making your moves at the right time.

Time management and efficiency gurus feed into the unsustainable grinder startup culture. On the other side of the scale are people who retire and say they get nothing done all day because they stretch out each task to the time they have available.

Contrary to what the productivity gurus will tell you, MegaWealth Timing is about balancing deep, effective work with space for strategic thinking. Rest and time away let your brain recharge in order to do its best work.

Time Blocking and Deep Work

When people hear how much I get done in a day, month, or year, they exclaim, "You must be an excellent multitasker!" Nothing could be further from the truth. I refuse to multitask as it wastes time making your brain shift from one activity to the next and back again.

For time management, I practice and suggest blocks of deep work. It normally takes me 15 minutes to get fully concentrated and 10 to come out of that concentration. I can work for 1.5-2.5 hours, so I set my deep work blocks to 2-3 hours. I work on one thing. You have to find the length of time and time of day that work best for you.

I typically have 1-3 blocks of deep work per day with at least 30 minutes in between to go for a walk, rest, or otherwise relax. For each block, I label it at least the night before as to what I will work on during that block. You may have areas like getting on boards or researching companies or industries that will take multiple blocks, so you can assign recurring blocks to those efforts until they are accomplished.

Using time blocking combined with deep work will accelerate your results towards your MegaWealth goal. How? While others are working on this and that, you are moving forward rapidly, making significant progress on your goals.

This progress compounds day in and day out. As time goes by, you'll be amazed at how far ahead you are compared to those you used to consider your peers. In order to keep going and to do your best work, you need to balance deep work and time blocking with periods of rest and relaxation. Why? It keeps you and your brain fresh, like a tune-up, so you can do your best work.

Periods of Rest and Reflection

Resting is not about being lazy. When I was young and working 80-100 hour weeks, which is sometimes necessary, I'd say, "I'll sleep when I'm dead." In a case of being careful what you wish for, I was hospitalized 3 times and my workmate 2 times in the final year of operation at Palantir Capital. My boss didn't push us. We pushed ourselves.

The crazy thing is that my best ideas come after a good night's sleep and normally when I am out on a walk, not sitting in front of a computer. Does this mean we should all sleep in and go for walks instead of work? Obviously not!

You push yourself, take in all the information possible, connect, question, learn, and then you'll see breakthroughs in your thinking when you rest and give your brain some space. I calendar in these rest periods, some for 30 minutes, some for 90 minutes. Find the cadence that helps you achieve your goals faster while staying in good mental and physical health.

Now that you know how to maximize your time each day, it's time to look at a different kind of timing that might be considered even more critical: timing your career moves.

Making Your Moves at the Right Time

Timing is most critical when making moves in your career. As I mentioned earlier, I advise clients to stay at each role for at least 3 years. While this advice is sometimes called "dated," the math stays the same: high-quality companies lose money for 6-12 months after they hire you because they invest in recruiting, training, and developing you. If a high-quality company sees that your work history is filled with 9-12 month roles, they won't hire you. As you execute on your MegaWealth Money Flywheel, with each Build position, you'll need to show results (e.g., grow sales from $10M to $50M) to then earn your next role. Getting traction and creating results takes time.

Aside from using time to accelerate your path to MegaWealth, time can influence your happiness. People often wonder why some rich people are happy and others are not. Why do all this work to try for MegaWealth if you'll end up miserable?

Of the 5 billionaires I have worked for and the many more I have known, time (calendar control) is one of the 3Cs that I see that drives happiness. The 3Cs are Calendar, Confidence, and Capital.

Control over your Capital is covered in Chapter 11 (investing). Control over your Confidence has many facets, but the MegaWealth Pyramid will give you an excellent foundation (Chapters 8 and 13). Control over your Calendar is something you can gain over time if you focus on that as a goal. Some friends of mine, who are worth more than $100 million, don't control their calendars while others with less wealth do.

When starting out, you may not have much calendar control. Try not to have calendar control guide which roles you take as you may trade away bigger opportunities. Be aware if you are building a life where, even as a wealthy person, you still won't have control over your calendar. How can you change this? Often, when we are doing something that goes against our happiness, it serves us in another way (victim mentality, avoidance, or something else). Reflect on whether you give up control of your time and how doing so may be serving you in some way. For me, I am a people pleaser. Having a full calendar gives me an easy "out" rather than having to directly turn people down or do things I don't want to.

Right now, go back over this chapter on time and timing. Where do you want to improve? Then, write down a plan. I find my clients' biggest gains come from instituting time blocking along with prioritization: work on the most important item first, and do it in a fully concentrated time block. I put these blocks in my calendar.

Try out this system along with NOT filling every moment of your day. If you feel compelled to fill every moment, then calendar in breaks. Breaks allow you to think deeply during your deep work. This is the essence of controlling your calendar.

Finally, use the 3Bs along with your analysis of the industry and company you are in to think about your ideal timing to move along your MegaWealth path. Chapters 10 and 14 will give you more details on how to do that analysis.

MegaWealth Timing Key Takeaways:

1. Use time blocking and deep work to massively improve your daily progress on any goals you set.

2. Your biggest breakthroughs will happen during periods of rest. That's how our brains work. Rest also helps strengthen the foundation of your pyramid, your health.

3. Timing your moves through the 3Bs and into the right industries and companies is the most difficult and most rewarding step of MegaWealth Timing. To get this right, combine the lessons in this chapter with those of Chapter 7 on industry, company, and timing. Remember, even if you don't time it perfectly, your money flywheel will give you a bigger surface area of opportunity to draw from.

The third critical component to success in building MegaWealth after mindset and timing is research. That is how you select the best companies and industries where you can build, invest, and advise.

CHAPTER 11: HOW TO BE A MEGAWEALTH INVESTOR: RESEARCH

Research is the 3rd critical component to success in reaching MegaWealth.

The results you get from beginner's luck can often look like the result of research, or even worse, fool you into thinking you're doing good research. Because I didn't learn how to research early enough in my investing journey, I consider myself both blessed and cursed with beginner's luck.

In my earliest years as an investor, starting at age 16, I had beginner's luck, a willingness to take risks, a dad who was a good investor, and the best timing imaginable. I had a dad who liked investing in small, risky stocks, and I was 16 in 1982, the moment the nation departed one of our deepest recessions and the stock market went into a raging bull market. Small, risky stocks do best in exactly this environment.

I turned $1,800 of savings into $320,000 in 4 years.

I don't recommend trying to repeat my beginner's luck or doing what I did (investing 100% of the money in one stock at a time, even when that meant having my entire $320,000 in one stock!). I was unwittingly benefitting from a system that came naturally to me. Later, through the patient teachings of my mentors and less patient lessons from Mr. Market, I built a system for investing.

How good is this system?

As I've shared before, I co-managed the #1 ranked Nicholas | Applegate Global Technology Fund, up 493% in 1999. Most funds were up big that year, but there's only one #1. The following year when NASDAQ was down 40%, I've already shared that I made my billionaire hedge fund boss hundreds of millions on one, single trade.

My investing system works for stocks, industries, and careers. From start to finish, it requires research.

1. Choose individual stocks to invest in.

2. Choose the industry and companies you'll join in your career.

3. Choose the private markets, industries, and companies to invest in (as an Angel, VC, and/or PE).

This framework can guide your choices on industries, companies, and timing of building, investing, and advising for your MegaWealth Money Flywheel.

Overview of my *Positive Change Investing System*

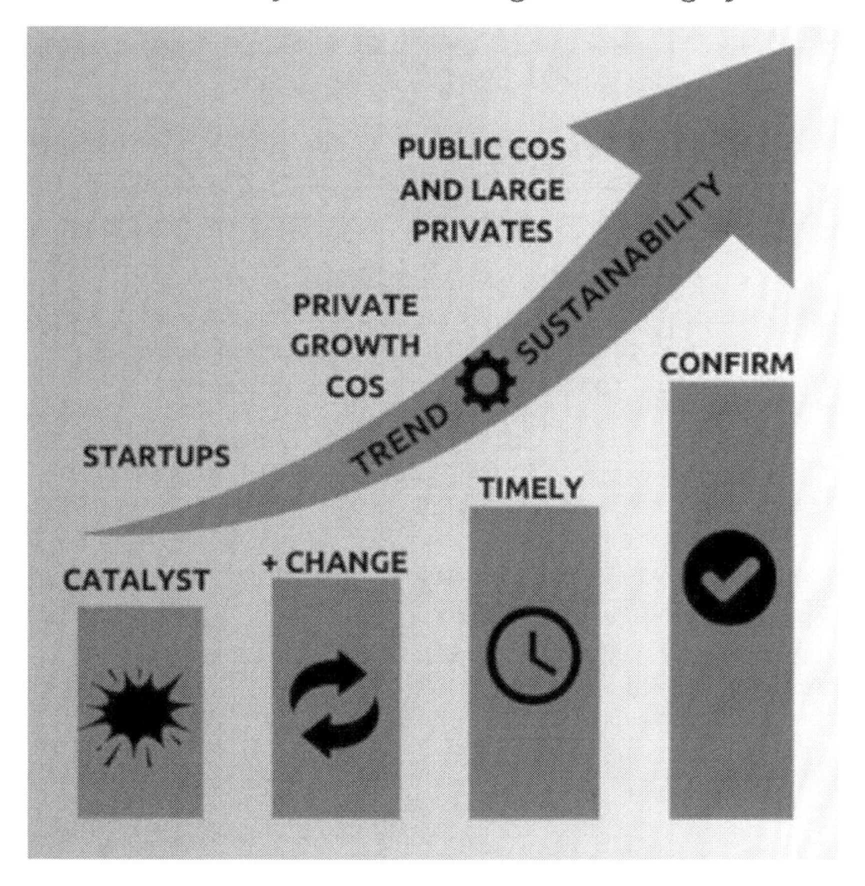

Here's how the Positive Change Investing System works:

1. Look for an Accelerating Catalyst

A catalyst can explain why a positive change might increase an industry's or company's growth rate. Observe promising industries with good industry dynamics and capacity for growth.

Keep an eye out for new regulations, new technologies, or changing demand patterns. These can all be positive catalysts.

Examples of positive catalysts include:

- The release of ChatGPT after decades of AI progress, which spurred massive investment in AI.
- The 1996 Telecom Act which broke up AT&T and launched thousands of internet businesses, powering the internet boom.
- People ordering everything online during COVID, changing their minds on what could be bought online, and thus drastically pulling forward our move to buying and working far more online.

2. Look for Positive Change Driven by the Accelerating Catalyst

Think back to the ideal situation: an industry is a fast-flowing river, and the ideal company to create or join is the fastest boat on the fastest river as long as the speed of both is sustainable.

In investing terms, that industry and company growth is being fueled by positive change, which is driven by an accelerating catalyst to create more demand, money, and market share.

3. Assess Catalyst Timeliness

Remember that existential question: "If a tree falls in a forest and no one hears it, did it happen?" Same goes for investing. Just because a company or industry experienced a positive catalyst doesn't mean investors are ready to take notice.

What if other investors don't see what you see? Is this your chance to get in early? Be careful! You may risk wasting years or even decades waiting for investors to see what you see. With your MegaWealth goal, these are years you can't afford to waste. Waiting will kill your compounding.

In private markets, AI technology was making great strides since the 1960s, but AI investing went through multiple heydays and investment winters. Only a few years ago, investors stated all the reasons why there would never be an AI "unicorn" (a company worth over $1 billion). As I mentioned above, the recent excitement and investing dollars started flowing into AI after the public introduction of ChatGPT, creating multiple unicorns in less than a year. Timing is everything!

4. Look for Confirmation

This is a tricky step. Don't get caught up in confirmation bias where you only look for new data that supports your thesis. What you are looking for, with the neutral mind you developed in Chapter 9, is to bring in data and assess if it is positive or negative, trying to be as detached to the answer as possible.

Lack of confirming data means that the positive change might not be sustainable. For a stock, you can sell it. For a company you joined, you may have to leave, so do more research ahead of time. For an angel investment in a private company, you may be in that investment far longer than the trend sustains.

5. Look for Unwinding (Signs of slowing when you should sell/exit)

Unwinding is when the elements you saw driving positive change start to reverse course. It is critical you mirror your analysis of when to enter or invest with your analysis of lack of confirmation of the sustainability of growth, followed by slowing, and when in this process you should sell or exit.

Nothing lasts forever. The faster the growth, the higher the risk that it won't sustain. Use your beginner mindset to ask open-ended questions. Use your neutral mindset to take in the answers. Listen for slowing at the margin, i.e., slightly less interested customers, less chatter about the topic where you were seeing excitement before, and other alternative products cropping up.

Some industries and companies go through temporary lulls before reaccelerating. With careers and private company investments, it is far harder to exit and re-enter, so stay calm, do more research upfront, but also don't overstay your welcome in an industry or company that starts to decline.

For the Unwinding, look for initial catalysts, confirmation, and assess how sustainable the decline is. It's a perfect mirror image of what you look for in an accelerating industry and company.

That's the Positive Change Investing System in a nutshell. To get the best results, you must do research using a beginner, neutral mindset.

One thing you may be wondering is how to find the fastest boat (company) on the fastest flowing river (industry). This is key for selecting your investments and where you invest the bulk of your time in your career.

Both industries and companies can be evaluated using the same system, which I introduced in Chapter 7 and will briefly revisit here.

An industry and company that can support your MegaWealth generation should have three main categories of characteristics.

MegaWealth: Attractive Industry and Company Characteristics

1. Large and Growing

An industry should be large or be able to become large. It should be growing faster than GDP (perhaps 5%-10% or more per year or faster for earlier emerging industries). Super-fast growth (50%-100%+) industries or companies may not be sustainable over more than a few years.

A company should be in a healthy, fast-growing industry. It is far riskier to think the company you are joining can create a brand-new industry or reinvigorate a dying one.

2. Healthy Competitive Dynamics

An industry and company should score well on Michael Porter's 5 forces, which is very similar to what Warren Buffett calls a moat:

- Not super price competitive
- No concentration of power on the part of buyers or suppliers
- Not many substitutes for the product because what the company or industry does is difficult or otherwise protected (patents, regulations, licenses)

3. Exhibiting Positive, Sustainable Change

Finally, an industry and company you are considering for investment or for your career choice should screen well in the Positive Change Investing System. It should possess the four elements my billionaire bosses looked for prior to investing:

- Positive Change
- Catalyst
- Timeliness
- Confirmation

All these lead to a higher chance that the growth you observe is sustainable.

How to Execute Your MegaWealth Investing

I've shown you my results and my process. Now, you need to make it your own. Markets, stocks, books, and mentors will add to your education. Listen to an interview of any experienced professional investor and they'll tell you they learn every day.

Here's how I recommend you start:

1. Invest in public equities

Invest 80% of the money you decide to allocate to equities into the general indices like the S&P through the most tax efficient vehicle (normally ETFs).

Take 20% of your equity allocation and invest in individual stocks by doing the kind of research I have indicated in this chapter and in Chapter 7. I highly recommend you stick to 1-2 industries you are interested in so you can learn about the players and become a better investor faster instead of picking individual stocks with no industry intelligence.

2. Learn from your mistakes

Mistakes are:

- Losses in your portfolio
- Lost profits from selling too early or too late
- Opportunity costs from keeping the slower-moving stocks and selling the better ones

Track what happens to stocks after you sell them and compare those returns to the returns of the stocks you kept. Reflect on and analyze your mistakes, your triumphs, and your lessons learned. Keep a journal.

Build your own system, which may use elements of my system but which you'll customize over time, given your personality, chosen industry, and experience.

3. Use this system for your career

Rather than reacting to recruiters or taking job offers for 20% pay increases, take a more strategic approach. What industry will fit well into your money flywheel such that there is healthy VC activity, good sustainability of growth, and is an industry you are interested in? This can be more than one industry. Which are the top companies in that industry?

Start networking with people who work at your target companies. Find ways to collaborate and get creative. You are now approaching your career like an investor. Your career is your biggest investment - time you'll never get back.

4. Apply your learnings to private markets

You'll have learned both from picking industries and stocks in public markets as well as doing deep research into the industries and companies you want to join as an employee and, later, a leader.

The next step is to take this research capability into private market investing as an angel investor, venture investor, and/or private equity investor.

How to Be a Private Market Investor

As part of your money flywheel, you'll be compensated with equity in private companies that you are helping to build or are advising or investing in. The moment you get equity in a private company alongside a reduced salary instead of the full salary you might receive at a larger company, you have become a private market investor.

Here are the main categories of private market investing relevant to your money flywheel:

Angel Investing

I used to joke that angel investing is an oxymoron because of the word investing. You have no idea if you'll ever see the money you put in. Angel investing refers to the earliest stage investors, typically friends and family of the founder, who are the only ones willing to give them money that early.

I have raised angel rounds for my startups. I can confirm that no matter who we reached out to (more than 300 in one raise), the people who wrote checks had known the founders for decades. Why? Because once they have your money, they can either build a company and succeed, try to build a company and fail, or just draw a salary from your money and go to the beach.

Angel investing is all about trust.

From an investing standpoint, remember, you can't sell your mistakes. You have to try and fix them or write them off. Take time to research far more than you would a public stock. Look for reasons to say no. Only invest in founders and teams you respect and want to spend time with because, more than likely, something will go wrong at some point and you'll be spending a lot more time together than you imagined. Working with teams has been both my greatest joy and largest source of stress, depending on the team.

What's potentially lucrative about angel investing? It only takes one great company to erase losses from other failures because you can earn 1,000X or 100X on your money. Be careful to contemplate how much your investment might return. You may get diluted by more investment dollars coming in from Venture Capital. Don't buy that second home with your 1,000X before it hits the bank.

90% of startups fail in 5 years. This sounds risky. It is. What if you don't want to be an angel investor?

If you are working in private markets for equity, you are already an angel investor. Angel investing outside your main Build role will give you practice selecting investments with smaller checks before garnering a role in either VC or PE. Most importantly, angel investing is a networking goldmine. You will meet great founders, investors, and board members. Nothing will bring you closer together than writing a check!

Venture Capital Investing

Remember those 100X and 1,000X returns? Venture capital relies on those to offset the fact that they are investing in startups, 90% of which fail. The dark side to VC is that they really PUSH founders to grow because they need those big winners. They have investors who push them. VC check sizes are bigger, with more pressure and risks, so it's great to learn the ropes as an angel investor.

The bright side of VC is the potential significant financial advantages of investing with other people's money at scale, getting a fee based on how much money they invest and tax deferring that fee as "carry" (i.e., the management fee becomes a larger share of fund ownership instead of taking cash payment from investors). This makes sense because these markets are illiquid, but it doesn't erase the fact that a large VC is a very lucrative endeavor.

How will you play in VC?

You can start as a Limited Partner (LP), which is an investor in a VC fund. I started in a smaller emerging fund where my friend was a general partner. She made the introduction. I was impressed with how they invested and with the backgrounds of the other partners. Don't worry, there are smaller funds where you won't have to write huge checks so you can build knowledge. Being a VC LP has given me incredible networking opportunities as I am sure it will do for you.

The second phase of your interactions with VCs will likely be as a leader in the private company you join as part of moving into your Building Equity phase. Network with these investors, and later, when they see you execute at your current company, they may ask you to lead one of their other promising portfolio companies.

The final way you can interact with VCs in the context of your money flywheel is first as a scout and later as a part-time partner. If you are becoming an expert in a vibrant industry as you Build, VCs will pay you to find and introduce them to exciting founders. One client I had ran a top technology podcast and was paid as a scout to introduce one VC to the founders he interviewed.

Once you are established enough in your industry, you may be asked to join a VC fund as a part-time partner where you are paid a minimal salary plus part of the profits of the fund. (The VC typically keeps 20% of fund profits, and this share of fund profits is called "carry.")

Venture capital investing starts at a very early seed stage, investing alongside angel investors, and goes all the way to huge growth companies which could be public companies but have chosen to stay private. The investors in larger, private companies are called growth equity investors.

Your money flywheel will be most effective if you first determine the stage of the company you want to join (early-stage, late-stage, pre-IPO, etc.). Then, network into VCs that are active in that stage of the company, and try to invest as an LP in VCs investing in that stage.

Quite often, you can see later-stage growth VCs investing side by side with private equity funds. This is why I advise my clients not to dismiss private equity as part of their money flywheel until they figure out the stage of the companies they want to work in.

Private Equity

Private Equity differs from Venture Capital in that they play with the entire cap table (equity, debt, receivables, and leverage) and are more deal-oriented. Because they often buy entire companies to take them private or combine them with other companies, the top private equity firms are typically larger than the top venture capital firms.

Why does the size of PE and their appetite for buying entire companies matter?

Once you have determined you want to be building in later-stage private companies, deciding whether to network into PE or VC will depend on yourself and them. Yourself because you have to look at your personality and passions. VC is more about growth and more growth. They benefit from the growth via their equity investment. Private equity may buy an entire company, combine it with 1-3 others in their portfolio, or leverage up the company and cut their costs, preparing it for an IPO. Private equity is more deal-oriented. If you love deals, numbers, and being creative with the entire cap table, PE may be a great choice for you.

However, make sure PE is ready for the industry you have chosen. Because these PE firms are bigger, their investments have to be larger in order to have the successful ones move the needle on overall firm performance. Make sure the timing of your industry having enough revenues per company matches with the minimum revenue requirements for PE. Otherwise, you'll be in an industry they don't invest in yet.

As I mentioned before, many PE firms invest side-by-side with growth equity VC investors, taking only a slice of equity or possibly providing some debt but not buying the entire company. Some of those PE firms are considered price takers, i.e., not the smartest money, but others are well respected. PE requires the largest confluence of events to go right in order to have it become a part of your money flywheel, but it still can be a powerful part if everything lines up.

Summary

MegaWealth Investing is about investing for high returns in both your investment portfolio and your career. By combining your career and your investing, you are strengthening both. This does not equate to putting all your eggs in one basket. Instead, you build a basket, or a flywheel, where each element makes the others stronger.

MegaWealth Investing Key Takeaways:

1. Use the Positive Change Investing System (PCIS) to research which public companies to invest in, then to research industries and private companies to join in order to Build Equity. Finally, use the PCIS to research which private companies to invest in as an angel investor and part-time VC or PE scout/partner.

2. Research and analyze the health of industries and companies using proven methods such as Porter's 5 Forces and Buffett's moat.

3. Navigate private markets using your money flywheel, seeing investing and advising as networking opportunities as well as wealth generation vehicles.

Congratulations on making it through Part 2 and learning how to build your money flywheel, navigate the 3Bs, remove any roadblocks using the Wealth Pyramid, and finally learning the critical components of the MegaWealth Mindset, MegaWealth Timing, and MegaWealth Investing that you'll need to have the most success.

In Part 3, I will show you how to build your own MegaWealth Plan.

PART 3: HOW TO DESIGN YOUR MEGAWEALTH PLAN

STOP! Before you go any further, download and print (for filling out) your

MegaWealth Plan PDF Workbook from Chapter 15: Resources. The next 3 chapters will guide you to answer questions on your way to building your MegaWealth Plan. The PDF workbook helps you keep all your answers organized in one place so that, in the end, you have an amazing document to refer to and your very own MegaWealth Plan.

Once you have downloaded the MegaWealth Workbook, keep it by your side and enter in your answers for the relevant sections as you go through this part of the book. You'll see it starts with Chapter 7, but don't worry if you are only downloading it now before Chapter 12. You didn't miss anything!

Chapter 7 introduces you to the ideas of how to find the right industry, company, and timing whereas the workbook has you go through specific exercises using that information.

If you want, you can read the book all the way through because the workbook gives you an outline of what the book says. Then, you can fill out the workbook once you are finished reading this book. Each of us works and learns differently. I set this up so you can pick the method that works best for you.

This PDF Workbook will guide you to:

1. Draft your money flywheel
2. Define your career path in the 3Bs Framework
3. Decide which roadblocks you need to remove
4. Design your personal MegaWealth Plan

As I'll explain in Chapters 12-14 of MegaWealth, this is a step-by step process. This workbook also contains excerpts from the MegaWealth book so you have context.

The best way to work with this PDF Workbook is:

1. Before reading Chapters 12-14, print or download the MegaWealth PDF Workbook.
2. Google instructions for accessing the accompanying PDF from the version you purchased (Amazon: Kindle, Audible, Paperback, Hardcover, etc.).
3. Read each chapter with the workbook by your side, answering questions and filling it out as you go along.

Don't worry if you don't have all the answers. I don't expect you to. This is meant to be a living document. Start with your best ideas, then keep adding to them over time. Remember, most people don't have a plan at all. You are already ahead!

CHAPTER 12: TOP TIP #1: DESIGN YOUR MONEY FLYWHEEL

When you use a map, you start with the destination, then find the route. Similarly, no matter where you are in the 3Bs (Breaking In, Building Equity, or Breaking Out), you need to start building your plan by designing your destination; your MegaWealth Money Flywheel.

Here's the typical money flywheel (which I've shared with you before) so you have it here for easy reference:

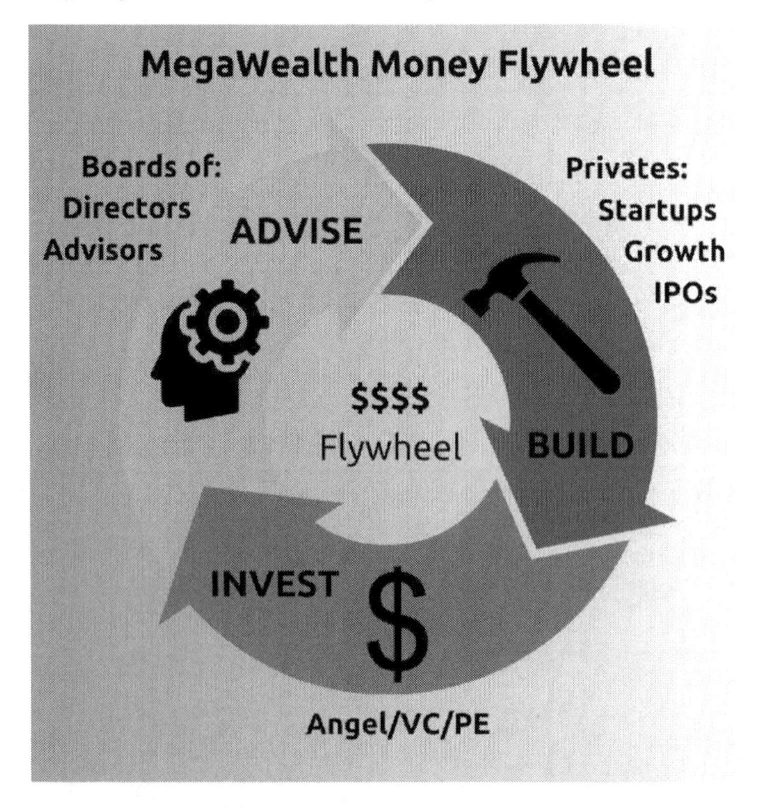

Just like copying someone's signature, the best way to do it is also the least obvious. (Copy a signature upside down to untrain your automatic movements.) When designing your final destination, which is your fully activated money flywheel, it would seem obvious to start with what type of company you'll build. Instead, we'll turn the paper upside down and start with Advise, Invest, and, finally, Build.

Advise

The advising portion of the MegaWealth Money Flywheel is the easiest to decide on *and* the hardest to execute. It's easiest to decide because it comes down to how formal of an advisor you want to be. It's the hardest to execute because you rely on others to reach out to you and ask you to be an advisor or board director, not the other way around. For those prone to action (which you need to be to go after MegaWealth), this is a hard pill to swallow.

Think of advising on a spectrum. I informally advise my friends who are in startups. This is from time to time and unpaid. I am formally an advisor for several startups where I do more work, help them out more, and I have a mix of an advisory fee plus some form of equity, depending on the situation.

Private companies typically start with a small board of directors. Then with each raise, the new lead investor adds a director to the board. They have to start small so as not to end up with a massive board by the time they IPO. Smaller startups are cash-strapped, so they may not have money to pay cash to advisors, but they also don't have money to hire expensive executives. So, they form advisory boards of experienced people they wish they could hire. Here, you are more likely to earn equity than cash.

Larger private companies may have more than one independent director, so there's more opportunity, and they have cash to pay you plus equity. Also, when we visit the Invest portion, you'll see that, as a part-time VC, you may be asked to be a board observer, board advisor, or board member for that VC in the companies where you are active. In the Build portion, you'll hone in on what industries you are focused on.

Because the Advise role requires people to reach out to you, you need to build a track record of success AND tell people about it (via LinkedIn, networking, a newsletter, a blog, and/or a podcast).

Self-Assessment: What kind of Advisor do you want to be?

Score yourself from 1-5 on each of the following questions (1 = disagree, 5 = agree) and add up your total score:

1. I enjoy a more formalized, organized process with meetings, slide decks, and successful people to strategize with.
2. I don't mind meetings, even all day, as long as they are with powerful, interesting people and they are efficiently run.
3. I prefer more strategic, competitive, and branding discussions rather than fundraising and worrying about how much financial runway is left.
4. I dislike the uncertainty of working with very early (years 1-3) startups, even if that means I miss out on some exciting ideas.

Advisor and/or on a Board of Advisors (4-9)

You don't mind the uncertainty of startups and prefer to avoid day-long, structured meetings. You are more suited to being an advisor or on a more formal board of advisors rather than a board of director role. This may be true for the stage of life you are in now, or it may be true due to your personality (my case). If you scored closer to 4, you might enjoy earlier-stage startups, and if you scored closer to 9, you might like to work with startups that have a bit of structure, possibly having completed their Series B round of funding.

Board Director (10-20)

You don't mind long meetings and even enjoy the structure more than the free-wheeling ways of early startups. Sharing ideas with other impressive and accomplished business people while helping to guide a company through its challenges sounds interesting. If you are closer to 20, although you may need to start with smaller companies, you may be happiest with larger, more established companies. If your score is closer to 10, then your sweet spot is likely a company that has done a few rounds of funding (Series B or C) but is still agile and hungry.

These learnings about what size of company you want to advise will serve you well as you decide on your Invest and Build portions. Your money flywheel will work best if you stay at the same stage of company (i.e., Series B-D, or A-C, or D-F) throughout your flywheel.

Now that you know where you want to be in Advise, how do you get there?

Throughout the Build portion of your money flywheel, you'll interact with board members of the company you are building while you rack up accomplishments for the company. Being instrumental in growing revenues will get you noticed most. Throughout the Invest portion of your money flywheel, you'll get to know other companies, other investors, and other board directors. They will see your accomplishments through your execution, networking, and thought leadership on professional social platforms like LinkedIn. And suddenly, you're exactly where you want to be as an advisor in a role best suited for you.

Invest

It may take a bit of time to learn an investing system and even more time to learn from market feedback what really works for you. Take a moment to reflect on where you might want to invest.

Investing Self-Assessment: Where do you want to engage?

Score yourself from 1-5 on each of the following questions (1 = disagree, 5 = agree) and add up your total score:

1. I did the work in this book on selecting attractive industries and companies. The industries I'm drawn to have strong growth but are more developed and less cutting-edge than others.

2. When I think about my personality and my answers to the Advise section, I realize that I prefer a balance of stability and growth. I think there are still plenty of opportunities for wealth generation with larger private companies.

3. It's no problem to start small, writing multiple checks as an angel investor, but in the end, I want to work on larger deals with companies that have established customer bases and growth plans.

Need for Speed (Score 3-6)

You'll start as an angel investor and likely fall in love with the small startup space. Here, the returns and the risks are high. You get the chance to envision and be part of a brand new future on a daily basis. It's not for the faint of heart, but neither are long meetings for some people. Do you!

Go Big or Go Home (Score 7-15)

You know yourself and prefer a bit more visibility while still having the opportunity for massive upsides. Look no further than later-stage VCs who log plenty of doubles with the occasional home run. They aren't plagued by the 90% startup failure rate like their early-stage counterparts. Preferring later-stage companies gives you the option to align with either growth VCs or Private Equity.

If you want to focus on later-stage companies and the previous Advise section showed you that you might end up enjoying being a board director, then your Invest plan should include networking into later-stage growth VCs and Private Equity companies who co-invest in these rounds. If you are more of a deal person and like thinking about how to maximize value using the entire capitalization table (debt, equity, receivables, and investor mix), then Private Equity might be more interesting to you than growth VC. This isn't about executing right now. It's about making a plan that says what you'll aim to do in the Invest portion of your money flywheel.

Build

When people think of building something in the business world, often the first thought is creating a startup. The biggest pushback I get from clients is "I don't know what to build."

Throughout this book, you've seen that the build stage is more than creating a startup from scratch. It's moving any private company from point A to point B and being able to show how you helped that company grow. In fact, big wealth gains, like we saw with Frank Slootman, CEO of Snowflake, can happen at the later-stage companies moving into IPO territory. You do need to build a reliable track record so you can command a large equity stake for your efforts.

You've started to circle what stage of a company you might be most interested in working with from the Invest and Advise perspectives. This will help you narrow down what you want to do in the Build portion of your money flywheel. You've also started looking into industries and companies that might be of interest.

How to decide what and where to build

1. Stage. What stage are you most comfortable at in the Advise and Invest sections? You can build at a company that is in a slightly earlier stage, but don't wander too far in that direction. Otherwise, the flywheel won't generate huge returns by having interactions between your Build, Invest, and Advise portions.

2. Industry. What industry do you have interest in where you have a background or can build knowledge and skills to develop a background in? I was a technology analyst for 25 years before moving into startups, and I did this by taking coding classes and starting my own small company to learn the ropes of sales, marketing, and operations.

3. Company. Find great companies in the industries you are interested in. Make lists of their competitors, suppliers, and customers. Get to know the industry dynamics and players. Check review sites to be sure you'd want to work there. Make a list of target companies to network into for opportunities.

Choosing a company to build with will get far easier as your money flywheel is activated. You'll have a track record of building, investing, and advising, all of which will mean new opportunities will come to you. Never let that stop you from redoing this process so you are proactively going after what you want rather than reactively accepting what is offered to you.

I purposely don't have a self-assessment in the Build phase. There are too many variables, and thus, the results wouldn't help your process. I know if you go through the three items listed above, you'll be able to come up with some great ideas of where and what you want to help build.

Chapter 12 Key Takeaways: Draw Your Money Flywheel in Your PDF

1. Advise - write down advisor or board director.
2. Invest - write down VC or PE and what stage is ideal for you.
3. Build - write down your target industry and 4 target companies.

Huge congrats! You have a clearer picture of your destination. Now, in the next chapter, let's remove potential roadblocks that might slow your progress.

CHAPTER 13: TOP TIP #2: REMOVING ROADBLOCKS USING YOUR MEGAWEALTH PYRAMID

Auditing your MegaWealth Pyramid will help you identify and remove roadblocks to your MegaWealth Plan. To help you do this, you'll answer the Wealth Pyramid questions I ask below to identify any potential foundational roadblocks to your plan, go to the relevant chapters to find a way to improve them, and add those improvement goals to your quarterly and annual plans.

The MegaWealth Pyramid helps you build your strongest foundation to be able to go as far as you desire and perhaps even farther than you dare dream is possible.

First, you set out your moonshot goal along with your money flywheel and 3Bs Framework map. Now, you are going to remove any obstacles to achieving those big goals.

Here's the MegaWealth Pyramid for removing roadblocks

(I include it here again for convenience)

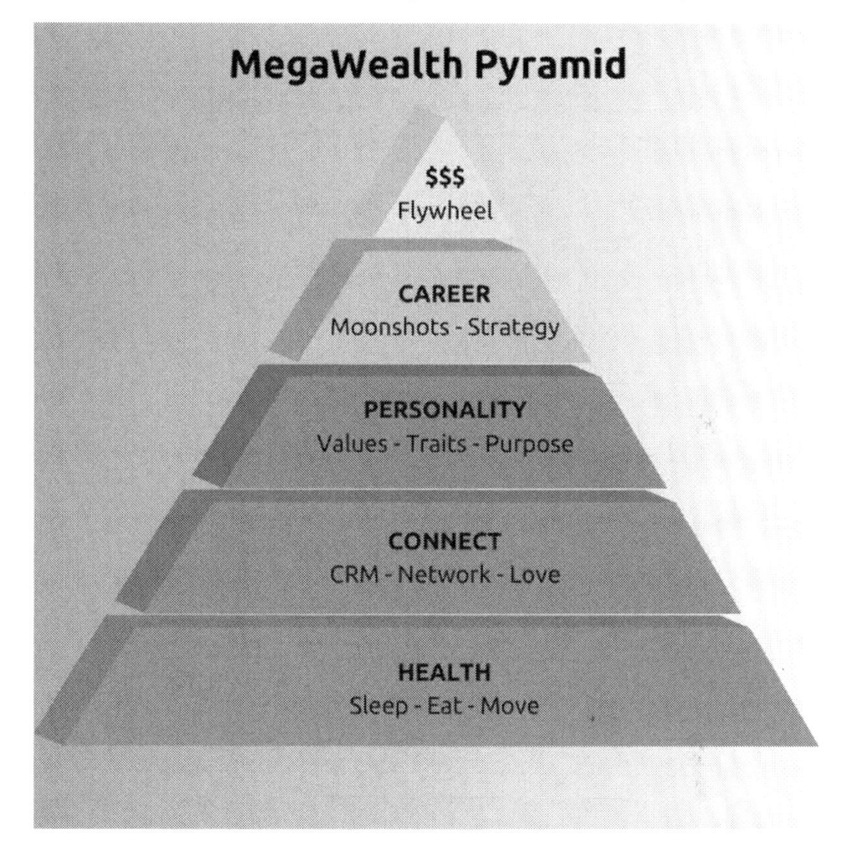

As I've mentioned previously, a pyramid is only as strong as its foundation. In each layer, starting from the bottom, you'll perform a self-assessment. If you have low scores you want to improve, you are not alone. Don't worry. I will give you resources every step of the way.

First, let's figure out where you are happy with where you are at and where you want to improve.

Foundational Layer 1: Health

Embarking on a multiyear to multidecade Wealth Plan which involves big goals and hard work requires stamina and good judgment. These come from a foundation of good sleep, nutrition, and exercise. You want to be healthy to enjoy the fruits of your labor!

To determine if there are any roadblocks in Health, ask yourself these questions.

1. How is your sleep (1-10)? How much do you want to improve your sleep (1-10)?
2. How is your nutrition, i.e., do you eat whole foods or junk foods? Are you happy with your weight? Do you have a healthy relationship with alcohol and drugs (1-10)? How much do you want to improve your nutrition (1-10)?
3. How is your exercise routine? Do you move regularly (1-10)? How much do you want to improve your exercise routine (1-10)?

<u>Results</u>: Order your 3 *Health* areas by which ones you want to improve the most as long as they still have room for improvement. Thus, if you score your exercise at 9, there's not much room for improvement, so focus on either sleep or nutrition, prioritizing low scores which you have a high desire to improve.

Foundational Layer 2: Connect

Networking can be overwhelming and scary, but it is the only way to get where you want to go. You can't go it alone. A major part of your mental and physical health is tied to feeling positive connections both personal and professional.

To determine if there are any roadblocks in Connect, ask yourself these questions.

1. How organized is your networking process, i.e., do you have a personal CRM (1-10)? How much do you want to improve your networking process (1-10)?
2. How deep, relevant, and useful is your network (1-10)? How much do you want to improve your network (1-10)?
3. How are your personal connections (friends, family, and love life)? Do you have the quality and quantity of relationships you want (1-10)? How much do you want to improve your personal connections (1-10)?

Results: In your MegaWealth Workbook PDF, order your 3 *Connect* areas by which ones you want to improve the most as long as they still have room for improvement. Thus, if your score in personal connections is 9, there's not much room for improvement, so focus on either building your work network or the process of networking and using your CRM, prioritizing low scores which you have a high desire to improve.

Foundational Layer 3: Personality

In order to have the most staying power and persistence in going after your goals, your personality (values, traits, and purpose) must be in alignment with where you are headed. This is the foundational step most of my clients want to skip. It's also the step that yields them, and will yield you, the greatest benefits.

First, perform a values audit.

The PDF provided in Chapter 15: Resources includes a list of typical values. You can also find more online. Pick words that speak to you. Write down other words that come to mind. Think of your favorite relative, your best childhood pet, or your favorite friend (then or now). Why are they your favorite? What qualities do they possess?

You should have 40 words written down of values you like in others and those you want in yourself. For instance, some of my top values are independence, generosity, love, positivity, and integrity. Yours may be different.

Any words that show up more than once should make it to the top of your list. First, rank order your values. Next, take a hard look and see if there are any values you want to remove or any you are living your life by that aren't serving you or may not serve you in the next phase of your life. Those at the bottom of the list can easily be dropped, whereas those higher up will require more reflection before replacing or dropping them.

Take the final list of values and rank order them once more, really focusing on your top 5 and top 10. Print out your top 5-10 and put them where you see them every day. Doing this will make your daily decisions far more likely to be in alignment with your values. Then, your decisions are easier to make, less likely to cause regret, and more likely to move you in your desired direction.

To determine if there are any roadblocks in Personality, ask yourself these questions:

1. How much do you live and act in accordance with your highest-ranked values (1-10)? How much do you want to improve your value-to-action alignment (1-10)?

2. How much do you possess the following startup executive traits: resilient, flexible, scaleable, action-oriented, and proactive not reactive (1-10)? How much do you want to improve your startup executive traits (1-10)?

3. How well aligned are your values and traits such that you have a clear sense of purpose (1-10)? How much do you want to improve your life purpose alignment with your values and traits (1-10)?

Results: Order your 3 *Personality* areas by which ones you want to improve the most as long as they still have room for improvement. Thus, if you score your startup executive traits at 9, there's not much room for improvement, so focus on either values or purpose, prioritizing low scores which you have a high desire to improve.

Clarity on your values, traits, and purpose will help you choose focus areas when building your own money flywheel.

Layer 4: Career

Finally, we are at the career layer. By the time you have your health, networking, and personality aligned, it is much easier to drive your career forward. The biggest challenge I see that stops people from building as much wealth as they could in their career is - they don't dream big enough.

Why is it so bad to underestimate our potential? Because you won't build big enough "moonshot" goals.

You need to *moonshot your career* because you don't have any idea how much more you are capable of than you think. It's not your fault. It's just that we humans think linearly, which way underestimates what we can each achieve in the long run. You also need to moonshot your career to avoid overachieving your goals and hitting that wall of demotivation.

To determine if there are any roadblocks in Career, ask yourself these questions:

1. How big are your goals and are they true moonshots (1-10)? How much do you want to improve the moonshot nature of your goals (1-10)?

2. How is your career strategy, i.e., is it clear, concise, and understandable (1-10)? How much do you want to improve your career strategy (1-10)?

Results: Order your 2 *Career* areas by which ones you want to improve the most as long as they still have room for improvement. My experience is that very few people have big enough moonshot goals, but you may be an exception. This book will help you lay out your strategy, step by step, once you have defined your moonshot goals.

Layer 5: $$$ Flywheel

Your MegaWealth Money Flywheel is at the top of your MegaWealth Pyramid. This is because if you have holes that need fixing in your foundation, executing on your money flywheel will be much harder or even impossible. If your flywheel isn't working, go back to your lower layers to figure out what's holding you back.

When your foundational layers are functioning well, you are healthy, energetic, connected, and your actions are aligned with your traits, values, and purpose. You know where you are headed. Building your flywheel becomes a natural extension of who you are and what you do.

You built your money flywheel in Chapter 12. Now, we are going to find and remove any obstacles that might hold you back from executing your MegaWealth Money Flywheel.

To determine if there are any roadblocks in Flywheel, ask yourself these questions:

1. How well aligned is your time spent in the 3 areas of your flywheel (Build, Invest, Advise) and your top strengths and skills (1-10)? How much do you want to improve your alignment (1-10)?

2. How many lower layers in your MegaWealth Pyramid do you need to improve to support your money flywheel (1-10)? How much will not improving these areas hold you back in building your money flywheel (1-10)?

Results: Order your 2 *Flywheel* areas by which ones you want to improve the most as long as they have room for improvement. Revisit the lower layers of the MegaWealth Pyramid, not to procrastinate but to be sure nothing critical is holding you back. This isn't about perfection. It's more like Occam's razor; make the most direct path to your goals while removing large obstacles in the way.

Now that your full, layer-by-layer audit is complete, you should be set up to execute on removing your largest obstacles and building the strongest foundation to achieve your moonshot goals using your money flywheel!

I know you can do it!

CHAPTER 14: TOP TIP #3: MAP YOUR MEGAWEALTH PLAN

You have envisioned your destination (the MegaWealth Money Flywheel) and identified roadblocks for removal using your MegaWealth Pyramid. Now, it's finally time to build your MegaWealth Plan.

Building out your plan will include 3 steps:

1. Name your end destination - the 3 parts of your Money Flywheel.
2. Name the roadblocks in your Wealth Pyramid you want to eliminate.
3. Map out where you are in the 3Bs and put everything in a sequential plan.

Step 1: Naming your end destination

Write down your best estimate, after some research, as to the industry, the companies, and the stage of growth and maturity of those companies you want to interact with. Do this for Advise, Invest, and Build. Now, write everything down as statements.

1. I will Advise as an Advisor/Board Director the following types of companies in the following industries. Fill in your answer in the PDF Workbook.
2. I will Invest as an angel in the following types of companies and industries while also working to gain a part-time role at a VC or PE firm which invests in

the following stages of companies, types of companies, and types of industries. Fill in your answer in the PDF Workbook.

3. I will Build and make measurable contributions to the growth of private companies in the following stage and industry. Fill in your answer in the PDF Workbook.

Step 2: Removing your roadblocks

Write down the list from Chapter 13 of all the roadblocks you identified in your MegaWealth Pyramid. As a reminder, these are items you scored yourself low on where you also scored high on wanting to change them.

Make an inventory of your areas of improvement, layer by layer.

1. <u>Health</u>: Sleep, eat, and move. List specific actions you'll take to improve the areas you want to improve.
2. <u>Connect</u>: CRM, network, and love. List specific actions you'll take to improve the areas you want to improve.
3. <u>Personality</u>: Values, traits, and purpose. List specific actions you'll take to improve the areas you want to refine. Pay particular attention to the alignment between your top 5 values and your top 5 desired traits to achieve your goals.
4. <u>Career</u>: Moonshots and strategy. List specific actions you'll take to improve the areas you want to improve.

Step 3: Building your plan

First, name your destination, i.e., what you will be working on and how your life will look specifically in 20 years, 10 years, and 5 years from now. Write out a paragraph for each, which can include what you are doing in terms of your money flywheel activities as well as family and other goals.

Everyone is different depending on how far out you want to plan. Perhaps you want to plan 30 years out instead of 20, for example. Yours could look like this:

20 Years

I will be on 3+ boards of directors, be an angel investor with 40+ lifetime investments, be a part-time partner at a top VC firm, and have built and exited 4 companies. I have a happy family life with friends outside of work. I am healthy and active.

10 Years

I will be on 1-2 boards of directors, advise several other startups, be an angel investor with 10+ lifetime investments, and have exited 1-2 companies where I was in a key leadership role.

5 Years

I will be on 1-2 boards of advisors and/or boards of directors, advise several other startups, be an angel investor with 5+ lifetime investments, and have exited 1 company where I was in a key leadership role.

Next, make a quarterly plan for the next 4 quarters (1 year)

You'll populate your interim goals, including removing your roadblocks. It could look like this:

Q1 2025:

Lay the foundation. Do the research. Get/read books, tools, and courses. Study paths you want to emulate of leaders in your industry. Make a plan of action for your priority areas like sleep, diet, networking, exercise, or whatever else cropped up in your Pyramid.

Research target industries, companies, and who their VC/PE investors are. Research what CRM you want to use. Remove sugar from your diet. Add 30 minutes of walking per day to each day. Organize your networking plan and start to fill out your CRM so you can systematize it.

Q2 2025:

Start researching the skills you'll need in the companies and industries you have decided on. Make a plan to add these needed skills through course work or experience. Use your CRM to network in a systematized way. Make plans for how many relevant people you'll meet each month and track your results. Now that you have your targeted industry and company and have done research, start sharing your views in a consistent way (3-5 times per week) on LinkedIn.

Set your priorities for implementation after research. Your action items could look like this:

1. 80% work IN your life. 20% work ON your life (planning, strategy, learning).
2. Start implementing your foundation CRM.
3. Start time blocking and doing deep work.
4. Spend 1 hour per week for long-term planning, reflection, and journaling. Spend 1-2 hours per week on professional social media creation.

5. Create a monthly and quarterly review cycle to track your top areas of improvement from your pyramid. (They could be sleep, diet, exercise, personal, and/or networking benchmarks.) Track progress against your goals.

6. Perhaps create a linktr.ee of your top links or your own website (I like Squarespace) which people also can use to get to know you better.

7. Position yourself for and accept public speaking gigs that support your Build, Invest, and Advise progress.

8. Network with VC and PE firms as well as their portfolio companies. You could also consult with a portco, showing progress to investors.

Q3 2025:

Consider how you might add value to the connections you are building in these industries or companies. What expertise or connections can you share? Keep building out your skills, network, and moving towards your goals. Your list for the third quarter could look like this:

1. Calendar regular check-ins with your new network using your CRM.

2. Outline and write your first book, establishing your thought leadership in a way that social media posting cannot. Think about what you want to speak about for the next 5-10 years that's at the intersection of where you are going professionally. Write about that.

3. Use 1 hour per week for long-term planning, reflection, and journaling.

4. Use 1.5 hours per week for social media and newsletter creation. Start promoting your book once it is in final draft form.

5. Consider starting a newsletter in your industry of interest. This should take 30-45 minutes per week. Add this time on to the hour you are writing social media posts.

6. Build a feedback loop of areas you want to improve and ways to measure them (they could be sleep, diet, exercise, personal, and/or networking benchmarks), and use your monthly and quarterly review cycle to track these areas against your goals.

Q4 2025:

1. Reflect on your progress. You have been using this system for almost a year. You are better known in your industry. You are timing the building of your money flywheel to best fit where you are in the 3Bs Framework.

2. Celebrate milestones. Your book may be out and you've been building your network and posting consistently on social media for over 6 months.

3. Continue with 1.5 hours on social networking and writing a newsletter and 1 hour for LT planning. Continue public speaking training and seeking public speaking opportunities. Perform regular network reach outs and continue your review cycles.

4. Keep networking with VC and PE firms about board seats and CxO opportunities, especially helping via paid consulting at relevant portcos while still continuing to build equity at your day job.

5. Depending on where you started, you may have the goal to be an advisor, board observer, or have a board role pending by YE25.

NOW you have one year of quarterly plans. Keep adding another quarter of plans as you move through each quarter.

Then, move to annual plans for the following two years:

2026

1. Perhaps you've been at the private company building equity and delivering significant traction for 2 years. You have moved up to a C-suite role or have delivered significant traction at your company such that you have offers for C-suite roles elsewhere. Balance trying to stay at each role for approximately 3 years to rack up accomplishments with moving to the next bigger opportunity.
2. You have built and formalized a tight relationship with 1-3 VC or PE firms and are seen as someone who can get into a business to energize growth. You have carry with at least one VC or PE firm. You are on at least one board and are perhaps observing on another.
3. Your money flywheel is activated!
4. Continue with your weekly 1.5 hours on social media and newsletter work (or hire a VA to run some of this), 1 hour of LT planning, public speaking training and seeking public speaking engagements, regular network reach outs, and review cycles.

2027

1. You are ready to exit your first private company role with significant equity gains.

2. Your next opportunity might be pre-IPO if you prefer to be in larger companies, or it may be starting at a company at an earlier stage where you can be awarded 5%-10% of the equity for a C-suite role. Design where you want to be and what kind of leadership you'll provide.

3. You choose your next opportunity with the visibility of having worked closely with your favorite VC or PE firms, being on boards, and having access to opportunities that only come with being in these networks.

4. This experience of leading either a pre-IPO and post-IPO public company or a smaller, high-growth company on a unicorn path sets you up for more lucrative board and leadership roles.

5. Continue with weekly work of spending 1.5 hours on social media and newsletter content (or hire a VA to run), 1 hour on LT planning, public speaking training and speaking engagements, regular network reach outs, and review cycles.

6. You launch your second book to stay top of mind, update your thinking based on what you've learned, and to support your next career goals.

Then, have a plan for 5 years out that could look like this:

2029

1. You are at the center of your chosen industry's discussions as a trusted leader, investor, and advisor. You are a true thought leader.

2. You have your second big exit, this time as part of the C-suite, perhaps via IPO if you chose the growth company route or by acquisition with you having a

bigger percent of the pie if you chose the smaller company route. You have the option to create your own family office to formalize your investing and leave a legacy.

3. You have the acumen and freedom to choose when to have zero debt or to add financial leverage, and with what proportion of your assets, to take advantage of opportunities and grow your wealth to the next level.

4. You have a large social following plus email subscribers and loyal book readers. You can launch a third book either in 2029 or 2030 as a precursor to the next steps in your career.

5. You have the choice of going ultra small and co-founding a startup with high caliber co-founders and VCs who know you or staying at a different stage of the company, perhaps taking a company through the IPO process and then leading a small public company.

Finally, have a plan for 10 years out that could look like this:

2034

1. You are wealthy, connected, powerful, and considered a person who gets things done.

2. You are known (through your networking, books, newsletter, and social media presence) by people of influence in your sphere and enjoy those you interact with.

3. You marvel at the fact that you are paid far more to work less hard than the average person on things

you greatly enjoy and with brilliant people! This is what having arrived is all about!

FINAL STEP: Using the PDF Workbook, make your own version of the above plan that takes into account where you are starting in the 3Bs Framework and your unique goals you want to accomplish in the end and along the way.

Chapter 14 Key Takeaways:

1. You have created your destination (your money flywheel) and removed your roadblocks. You have entered everything into your own plan, including quarterly and annual goals as well as a blueprint for 5 and 10 years in the future.

2. Once you have your plan, start executing and don't forget to take time to reflect on your wins and progress against your plan.

3. Remember, this plan is a living document, so as you exceed in some areas and take longer in other areas, update your plan.

4. As you start to work in private companies, you'll get a better idea of the size and type of company and industry you want to be in. Feel free to change your end goals, but try not to change your destination too often.

Congrats! You have built a plan few people have even ever considered building. Now, you can work towards your huge goals proactively and with purpose in order to build the most amazing life possible.

Conclusion

Congrats! You've made it! Thank you for joining me on this journey. I hope it's a strong beginning for your journey to MegaWealth!

You audited your life using the MegaWealth Pyramid. You figured out where you are and where you want to go using the 3Bs Framework, and you know how to get there since you designed your MegaWealth Money Flywheel. This puts you ahead of 99% of your peers!

Here's what you've learned and accomplished by reading this book:

1. The Silicon Valley Secret Key to MegaWealth is building a MegaWealth Money Flywheel.

2. Before you design your MegaWealth Money Flywheel, you need to first select the industry and companies you want to focus on and start thinking about how you'll time your move.

3. The first step to building your MegaWealth Money Flywheel is knowing where you are and where you want to go by using the 3Bs Framework (Breaking In, Building Equity, Breaking Out).

4. Next, you need to remove any roadblocks by using the MegaWealth Pyramid, starting with a foundation of strong health and connections.

5. Your work designing your money flywheel, knowing where you are in the 3Bs, and removing roadblocks are all critical components that will help you build your MegaWealth Plan.

6. But first, there are 3 critical components you need to master before you design your MegaWealth Plan.

7. The first critical component is your MegaWealth Mindset. The four mindsets that can help you most on your path to MegaWealth are the beginner mind, the neutral mind, the present mind, and the connected mind.

8. The second critical component is your MegaWealth Timing. Mastering your timing covers micro (how to schedule your day, give yourself breaks, and control your calendar) and macro (how to time your career moves).

9. The third critical component is your MegaWealth Investing. While you want to earn strong financial returns from every investment, MegaWealth Investing with an activated MegaWealth Money Flywheel means that your investments are also powerful networking tools.

10. Finally, after building this strong foundation of understanding, you are ready to build your MegaWealth Plan using the included PDF Workbook in the Resources chapter. Using this PDF, you accomplished the following:

    a. You designed your MegaWealth Money Flywheel (your end destination).

    b. You identified and made plans to remove your roadblocks using the MegaWealth Pyramid.

    c. You figured out where you are and what you need to do to get to your final destination using the 3Bs Framework.

    d. You wrote out your own customized MegaWealth Plan.

As you can see, you have everything you need to build a MegaWealth Plan. You have every tool and every strategy. I laid it all out on the table. As I mentioned earlier, it is clear, even simple, but it is not easy to go it alone.

If you want...

You can reach out to my team - learn more about what we do and how we could help you personally to architect your perfect MegaWealth Plan, Money Flywheel, and Wealth Pyramid all in the context of where you are in the 3Bs. This gets you on your new plan faster and with higher precision, leveraging my years of experience working with billionaires and seeing multiple friends make $100 million by age 50. I take all this expertise and apply it to your situation. This gets you where you want to be...

This book contains all my best information, but if you want customized advice from me, informed by years of working with billionaires, building my own money flywheel, and coaching others in your situation, I offer both coaching packages and hourly coaching, depending on what is the best fit for your needs. You can book a call to learn how I can help you here: https://calendly.com/emmy-sobieski/15-minute-intro-call

CHAPTER 15: RESOURCES

Download your MegaWealth PDF Workbook on Amazon or www.emmysobieski.com to complete your MegaWealth Plan using Chapters 12-14.

Have questions about this book?

Message me on LinkedIn and I will reply. If you prefer email, sign up for my MegaWealth Newsletter. Reply to one of my emails, and I will write you back.

Additional Free Resources:

I post daily tips on LinkedIn and Twitter. Sign up for my MegaWealth Newsletter. Additionally, I have videos on YouTube and have been a regular podcast guest, sharing my insights. Links and more resources are all available on www.emmysobieski.com.

My Online Courses to Help You Remove Roadblocks

Maybe your work on your MegaWealth Pyramid reveals areas you would like to improve around health, executive skills, networking, or social media and video presence. I offer courses for leveling up those skills: https://courses.emmysobieski.com/

Working with Me

If you decide you'd really rather speak with me and learn more about how I might help you, feel free to schedule a call here: https://calendly.com/emmy-sobieski/15-minute-intro-call

A FEW WORDS FROM THE AUTHOR

There are 720 Billionaires in the US. I have worked for five of them for over a decade. I made one $100 million in one trade and another $24 million in a year. I've seen firsthand how the ultra-wealthy build and keep their wealth and how they operate differently from the rest of us.

I mentored multiple underprivileged students to build net worths in the millions by age 30. I saw several friends hit $100 million in wealth by age 50. I ran the #1 Fund in 1999 up 493% (Nicholas | Applegate Global Technology Fund). I worked for the most exclusive hedge fund manager of the 1990s.

I've built equity in multiple companies through advising, operating, and investing. I founded, co-founded, or was a founding member of 7 companies (in green energy, blockchain/Web3, education, and finance).

During this time, I was world or nationally ranked in 3 sports (Bodybuilding, Sprinting, and Dressage) all after age 39. I've run 15 marathons and 6 ultramarathons starting at age 46.

However, I took a roundabout route to my own wealth. I had Ivy grades, went the State route, and spent my early 20s as a horse trainer. My first job after earning my MBA at USC was working in the bond department of an insurance company, making the equivalent of $10/hour (on salary). I failed to dream big enough. I didn't moonshot my career goals, so I overshot my smaller goals and stalled. I missed multiple onramps to the fast lane of wealth yet recovered. There are always second chances to get back on track.

I learned from my mistakes, my successes, and the success of my billionaire bosses, friends, and clients.

Now, I help highly motivated professionals map and execute their MegaWealth Plans as the MegaWealth Coach.

Made in the USA
Columbia, SC
27 May 2024